For Judy, 1943-1970—wherever

Books by Edward Abbey

BLACK SUN
FIRE ON THE MOUNTAIN
THE BRAVE COWBOY*
DESERT SOLITAIRE
JONATHAN TROY
THE MONKEY WRENCH GANG
THE JOURNEY HOME
ABBEY'S ROAD
GOOD NEWS

* Filmed as *Lonely Are The Brave*

Black Sun

A NOVEL BY
EDWARD ABBEY

CAPRA PRESS
Santa Barbara
1981

Copyright © 1971, 1981 by Edward Abbey.
First published by Simon & Schuster, 1971.
All rights reserved.
Printed in the United States of America.

Cover design by Terri Wright.

LIBRARY OF CONGRESS CATALOGING IN PUBLICATION DATA

Abbey, Edward, 1927-
   Black Sun.
   I. Title.

PS3551.B2B56   1981   813'.54   80-27953
ISBN 0-88496-192-3

Line on page 133, quoted from Robert Creeley's "For Love," used by permission of the publisher, Charles Scribner's Sons.

CAPRA PRESS
Post Office Box 2068
Santa Barbara, California 93120

Preface

Yes, yes, it's true, I fell in love with the great American West long ago, in the summer of '44, while floating through the desert and the mountains in a sidedoor Pullman. In a boxcar. On the Atchison, Topeka and Santa Fe (Holy Faith) Railroad. Jailed for vagrancy in Flagstaff, Arizona, robbed in Sacramento (the sacrament), California, mighty near sweated to death on a wheat ranch in South Dakota, left for dead in a ditch in the Idaho Panhandle, I survived all the same to fall in love. Permanently.

BLACK SUN is a novel about love. And about sex, and the forest, and love under the sun in the forest, and about disappearance. The vanishing of the loved one. About mystery, that is, and the bewildering grief of death. Like most honest novels, it is partly autobiographical, mostly invention, and entirely true. I wrote this book in four weeks, hacking away on a borrowed typewriter, at night, after work, in a strange place in Arizona.

Yes, and I have spent many a summer in what the Forest Service calls a "fire lookout." A tower in the woods. Far away from all that sustains sanity. The voice that speaks in this book is the passionate voice of the forest, that sound the wind makes wailing through the yellowpines. You'll see what I mean. The madness of desire, and the joy of love, and the anguish of final loss—so much, and no more, was my modest ambition in the creation of this book BLACK SUN. In my imagination, through ways incomprehensible to the author, desire and love and death lead through the wilderness of human life into the wilderness of the natural world—and continue, round and round, perhaps forever, back again to wherever it is we begin.

Pretentious words. Actually this book was written mostly for pleasure, for the pleasure of the sounds and the images, and if it is at all successful, then the reader will experience an analogous pleasure to that which I felt in the writing of it. Is not this the essential function of art, to add something if possible to the sum total of pleasure and form in a world where so much is subtracted by pain, confusion, fear?

EDWARD ABBEY
Oracle, Arizona, 1981

CONTENTS

PART I
IN THE FOREST   9

PART II
IN THE SUN   57

PART III
IN THE EVENING   125

There be three things which are too wonderful for me, yea, four which I know not:

The way of an eagle in the air; the way of a serpent upon a rock; the way of a ship in the midst of the sea; and the way of a man with a maid.

—*Proverbs*

PART I
In the Forest

1

EACH DAY BEGINS like any other. Gently. Cautiously. The way he likes it. A dawn wind through the forest, the questioning calls of obscure birds. He hears the flutelike song, cool as silver, of a hermit thrush.

He waits for a while, hands under his head, watching the light beyond the open doorway of the cabin. The subtle, stealthy shift from violet and blue to morning gray. He opens his sleeping bag, rolls off the bed and walks naked to the door, where he stands for some indefinable length of time gazing out, leaning against the doorframe.

The sun is close but not yet up. A few dim stars still hang blinking on the west. Deer are grazing at the far side of the clearing, near the foot of the fire tower—dim figures in the pearl-gray light. The dark and somber forest surrounds them all with its heavy stillness.

At last the man stirs himself and goes out, naked and barefooted, to the pump mounted on a cistern beside the cabin. The deer become shadows among the trees. He primes the pump, an archaic thing of cast iron and wood, and fills a bucket with cold melted snow water. Just beyond the edge of the clearing, under the dense shade of spruce and fir, are the surviving drifts and dunes of old snow which provide his water. When the snow is gone the rains will come to replenish the cistern by way of cabin roof and drainpipe. Here on the summit of a great plateau, miles from the nearest well, spring or stream, there is no other source.

Taking the bucket of water into the cabin, he builds a fire in the stove, fills the coffeepot. Smoke idles up from cracks in the old iron, the flames mutter, the hot draft rumbles quietly up the stovepipe and the smoke is gone.

He closes the damper on the stove and turns around to warm his backside, rubbing his belly, staring at nothing.

A mouse creeps from its nest beneath the cupboard, stops to stare up at the man, then scurries along the wall to a corner under the table. Stops again, watching. The man goes outside.

A tin basin hangs on a nail in the wall. He fills it at the pump and splashes the freezing water over his head and arms, over his chest. The air is still now, without a trace of motion. Grand broad and golden columns of sunlight slant through the aisles of the forest into the clearing. Shivering, he hurries back to the cabin and the stove and rubs himself dry with a big towel no longer so clean as it once was, perhaps, but cleaner than you might expect of a man living alone in the woods for half of every year. He pours himself a cupful of black, smoking, rich and murderous coffee and then, standing by the fire, still naked, staring at nothing, forgets to drink it.

This world is very quiet. Almost silent. The clear song of the hermit thrush exaggerates the stillness, makes it seem only more stark. If he were listening the man could hear the murmur of the fire in the stove, the creak of the metal roof expanding slightly in the first sunlight, the fall of a spruce cone on the ground outside. But nothing else. Later in the season—soon enough—will come other sounds: the thunder of lightning splitting the sky, spiraling like a snake in flame down the trunk of a tree, driving a cannonball of fire through the forest's carpet of dust, duff, debris—the sigh of burning trees, the roar of chaos. But now, nothing.

The mouse, stirring hungrily under the table, reminds the man of the alleged reality of present time. He drinks his coffee, puts on some clothes, an old coat, refills the mug and goes outside to the tower. In the chilly air steam rises from the hot coffee in his hand.

The tower is an open skeleton of steel, ninety feet high, tall enough to clear the highest trees in the vicinity. He climbs steadily up the wooden stairways, which rise in steep pitches from landing to landing inside the four legs of the tower. At the top is a single room with windows all around and a railed catwalk on the outside.

The uppermost flight of stairs brings him onto the catwalk. He leans against the wall on the sunny side, breathing heavily, sips at the steaming coffee and gazes out at the morning.

The tower is surrounded by the forest. In all directions lies the sea of treetops, a seemingly unbroken canopy of aspen and conifer rolling toward deserts in the dawn, toward snow-covered mountains far to the south and west, and on the remaining side toward something strange, a great cleft dividing the plateau from end to end, an abyss where the pale limestone walls of the rim fall off into a haze of shadows, and the shadows down into a deeper darkness.

There is nothing out there which is new to him, nothing which is wholly unknown. And yet, each time he climbs this tower, each time he looks out upon this world, it seems to him more alien and dreamlike than before. And, all of it, utterly empty.

2

One day there had been visitors. He was chopping wood, splitting blocks of aspen cleanly and sharply on a stump near the cabin. The ax blade gleamed in the sunlight, rising and falling. The chunks of wood, well-cured, fell apart under the blade without resistance, split and dropped and lay in a growing pile about the stump.

He heard voices but did not halt in his work. He often heard voices in this part of the forest. The fine leaves of the aspens, delicately suspended, shimmered like water under light, shivered and tinkled like glass bells with the slightest breeze, and their rustling taken all together resembled the whispering of voices, murmurs, speech without words.

Gathering his work in his arms, he heard now not voices but a single voice, the voice of a girl, answered at once by the voice of a young man and the voice of another girl. Down in the woods three people were coming up the path. He could not see them as yet, they were below the knoll and hidden by the trees.

He carried the kindling into the cabin, dropped it in the woodbox. Preparing for guests, he moved the coffeepot to the hottest part of the stove; he put on a clean shirt and lit his pipe and went out.

They came up the path, talking, smiling, and paused at the edge of the clearing for a moment when they saw him emerge from the cabin. Still buttoning his shirt. They came close. The young man put out his hand.

"Hello," he said. "We're from the lodge. We weren't sure you'd be up here so early in the year. Are you Mr. Gatlin?"

"Yes."

Shaking hands, the young man gave his own name, which Gatlin at once forgot, and introduced the girls. One was tall, solid, an athletic blonde with gleaming eyes and sharp features and bright perfect teeth with a fine cutting edge to them, exposed briefly in a wide and lavish smile. She wore a close-fitting suit of the cowgirl type; she looked very much like a rodeo queen or a homecoming princess. On the high heels of her boots she stood nearly as tall as

Gatlin and three or four inches taller than her young man. The elastic and lustrous fabric of her costume stretched without wrinkles over the splendid swell of her breasts and buttocks and generous thighs. Her name was Gloria Hollenbeck.

The other girl, a slim, quiet person in a kilt and sweater, was Sandy. She had sun-bleached coppery hair, very long, and freckles on her sunburned nose.

They wanted to climb the tower, see the inside.

He led them up the stairway. Out of habit he climbed at his usual pace and only the smaller girl, Sandy, seemed able to keep up with him. They halted near the top to wait for the others.

"It's very beautiful here. You must love it very much."

"Yes."

"Of course you don't live here all year round, do you?"

"No."

Breathing hard, the rodeo queen and the young man joined them on the landing. Gatlin went on, up two more flights to the catwalk and into the bright sun-warmed room. He opened some of the vents under the ceiling. The three visitors wandered around on the catwalk, looked down on the trees, looked far away at the mountains, the desert, the canyon. Gatlin switched on the shortwave radio, tuned out the roar of the squelch, turned up the volume. Silence.

He squeezed the button on the microphone and a red bulb glowed on the set.

"K.O.G. seven eighty-one, ten eight."

The radio muttered, preparing a reply. "Seven eighty-one, this is seven eighty. How's she look up there today, Will?"

Gatlin gazed through the glass at the shining figure of the rodeo queen. "Looks good, Wendell."

"Ten four. Seven eighty."

"Seven eighty-one."

His visitors entered. He showed them the radio sets, the weather recording instruments, the insulated chair for lightning storms, the maps that unrolled from mountings on the ceiling and, in the center of the room, on its high platform, the Osborne firefinder. He explained the operation of this device to the girls, showing them how to fix on a distant point through the peepsight and crosshairs, how to measure the vertical angle, how to read the vernier scale, how to match objects in the landscape with coordinates on the map. The young man was busy with Gatlin's binoculars, searching the forest for a trace of smoke.

"My God," Miss Hollenbeck said, "how complicated."

"It ain't much."

"You certainly keep everything nice and neat in here."

He said nothing.

She stared at him. "Don't you get awfully lonesome out here?"

"Sometimes."

"I'll bet. My God."

"Hey," the young man shouted, "I see a fire." He was staring through the field glasses at something in the south. "A big one."

"Let me see," the rodeo queen demanded, tugging at the binoculars. The young man yielded them to her without a struggle. She looked. "I can't see a thing."

Gatlin looked where the others were looking, said nothing.

"Should I try to get a reading on that fire?" the young man asked.

"It's not a fire."

"That's an awful lot of smoke."

"Dust."

"What?"

16

"Dust."

"How can you tell? That looks like smoke."

"It's dust."

"Well, I don't know, if I was you I think I'd report that anyway."

The girls watched him. Gatlin said nothing.

"Aren't you going to report it?"

"No."

The radio was crackling. An old man's voice came out of the speaker. "Seven eighty, seven eighty-six, got a smoke at two hundred and sixty-five degrees, about five miles from here. Looks big."

Gatlin took a reading on the dust cloud. After a few seconds another voice on the radio: "Seven eighty-one, seven eighty."

"Seven eighty-one," Gatlin said.

"Will, what do you see down that way?"

"A little dust at a hundred and seventy-nine degrees and six minutes. Twelve miles from here."

"Ten four. Stand by, please."

The radio went silent for a minute, then spoke. "Ten four, Will, they're bulldozing a stock tank in there. Seven eighty-six, did you read?"

"Ten four," the old man said.

Gatlin picked up the microphone. "K.O.G. seven eighty-one, ten seven." He shut off the radio. They watched him. "How about some coffee?" he said.

3

IN THE EVENINGS, through the leaf-filtered twilight, he walks down the path, swinging his stick, singing.

> "Every lassie has her laddie,
> None they say have I,
> But a' the lads they lie on me
> When comin' in the rye."

A bat flickers by on naked, pink translucent wings. Like a flying fetus. With teeth out and ears upright, with a face from Hieronymus Bosch. And spotted toads sing from the marsh below, tragically. Dirge for the dying day, lament for love. Dark birds flit silently through the pale glades of aspen, melt into darkness under boughs of spruce. Far off, one sad feathered fowl croaks dismally.

The path is soft, lushly carpeted with last year's leaves, damp from the melted snow. His big lug-soled boots make no sound. He sings the other song.

> "The gloomy night before us flies,
> The reign of terror now is o'er;
> Its gags, inquisitors and spies,
> Its hags and harpies are no more."

Descending, he enters a grove of yellow pine. The straight great trunks rise up toward asymmetric branches and the clouds of evening. Amber ships, violet sea. The grandeur of a world where tall trees stand under passing forms of golden vapor. Banks of crusted snow covered with dust and dusty pine needles glow dimly in the shadows at his side. Darkness below, light overhead, the soft air before him.

In the forest are deer, and coyote, and a few black bear, and the rare far-ranging mountain lion. And himself. His name? his name? Reaching out, he caresses as he passes the rough rugged bark of a pine.

The trail ends at the beginning of a road. Or the end of a road. His machine is here, the small jeep truck in a shed, that truck which looks as if it had survived not merely the wars of North Africa and the mud of Italy, but had been driven back to America by way of Tashkent and Samarkand, over the Burma Road and then towed beneath the Pacific by submarine and beached somewhere on the desert shore of Baja California, abandoned for twenty years, discovered, rehabilitated, brought finally home.

Fifteen miles to the village, the lodge, the store. The key is in the switch, where it belongs, where he always leaves it.

4

BUT STILL, perhaps, after all, the mornings are best. Coming down from the tower after that first survey, he goes to the nearest surviving snowbank under the dense growth of spruce. Buried in the snow is an ice chest, his refrigerator, which he opens. He takes out a slab of bacon, eggs, a covered dish containing three boiled potatoes.

Appetite rises, then hunger. Fire low in the stove, he adds fuel, removes a stove lid and sets his big cast-iron skillet directly on the opening. Not much left of the bacon; he draws the knife from its sheath on his belt and carves the slab into four thick slices, drops them into the skillet. He breaks the last of his eggs into a bowl, chops up a canful of green chili and stirs the bits into the eggs. Green and yellow, a pleasing blend. When the bacon is done he takes it out of the skillet and pours his eggs and chili mixture into the sputtering grease. A mighty pancake of an omelet begins to form at once. In a second, smaller pan, the potatoes, sliced and diced, are frying. Happily.

He pours the coffee. He peels an orange and drops the peelings into the woodbox; when dry, they'll burn. Under the cupboard the mouse is stirring again. He'll be fed. A squirrel is scratching its claws on the cabin roof. Looking out the window, he can see three does and a pair of fawns licking at a log where he had urinated earlier. Salt. There is a pecking order among the deer and the biggest, strongest of the does repeatedly drives off the others, striking out with its forelegs and sharp hoofs. But each time this happens the fawns slink in for a quick lick at the log. Two chipmunks come in through the open doorway and take up positions near the table, waiting for their share. Watching Gatlin eagerly, they rub their noses, preening, and switch their tails nervously, electrically back and forth, back and forth.

"Go home," he says, sitting down to his breakfast. "Go find your mother, for godsake. Little beggars."

But he lets a few crumbs fall to the floor, feels the chipmunks scrambling between his bare feet. He thinks of rabies, vaguely. In its nest under the cupboard the domesticated mouse stirs in restless, futile anger.

After breakfast he leans back in his chair, tilting it on two legs, puts his feet on the table or sometimes, if cold, on the open oven door. He cleans, fills, lights a pipe. Lets the fire die in the stove and listens to the development of the morning.

The cabin is one sparsely furnished room—the iron cook stove, table, two wooden chairs, an old bed. An extra cot, folded, rests against the wall. There is Gatlin's trunk. There is a pack frame hanging on the wall, and an old felt hat, and a Levi jacket, and a raincoat. Leaning in one corner are a deer rifle and a double-barreled shotgun. A lantern hangs by a loop of bailing wire from one of the rafters. There is the cupboard, and shelves braced to a wall, on which rest his personal treasures: pipes, tobacco, a chess set, a few stained broken-backed books, stationery, an open jar holding pens and pencils. Some photographs tacked above his bed—two women, the faces of children. On another shelf near the stove are his toothbrush, a comb, a straight razor in a leather case, a pocket mirror of stainless steel.

No calendar, no clock, no radio, no magazines, no newspapers.

No telephone. No doorbell.

No mailbox.

He climbs the tower again, checks in by radio with headquarters, the fire control center, and for an hour or more by the sun paces the catwalk, binoculars in hand, studying the silent forest, the distant canyons and ridges, the skyline. The forest is dry now, this forest is nearly always dry, always flammable, but until the lightning storms of July and August begin, the danger of fire is moderate. Most fires in this season are man-caused, and few men stray beyond the end of the roads.

He makes weather observations. Why not? He records the current temperature, the maximum and minimum temperatures for the past twenty-four hours, the relative humidity, the average wind speed, the precipitation (none for a month). He weighs some balsa sticks which are kept on a wire rack a few inches above a bed of pine needles and obtains a figure which is used in estimating the approximate moisture content of the forest floor and the consequent probable fire danger. He radios his data to the fire control center and goes out on the catwalk for another survey of the forest, looking for that little twist of gray, that wisp of blue which signifies woodsmoke and fire. Satisfied that the plateau or what he can see of it is clear, he props a chair against the wall, in the sun, lifts his feet to the rail and opens a fat book.

5

A SMALL MEADOW. At the upper end stands a glade of aspen trees with quaking leaves, straight slim trunks, the bark vestal white. Beyond the aspens, the darker forest of pine, fir, spruce. A flash of red bisects the darkness, vanishes.

He was drinking from an old wooden water trough below the spring where the wagon trail once led. The trough nothing but a hollowed-out log, the spring only a trickle caught in an earthen dam and guided through a rusty pipe into the log. But the water was clear and cold and sweet. Gazing into it as the circles widened around the drops that fell from his hands, he saw her smiling reflection rise beside his. The sunlight shone through her hair. He felt her hands move up his back, onto his shoulders, into his hair. She started to laugh.

6

"GATLIN, YOU BUM, where the hell are you?"

The great voice thunders through the woods as Art Ballantine marches into the clearing. Red curls on his forehead, a red fat neck, the curly hairs of his chest revealed in the open collar above the loosened tie. Panting from the climb, he strides to the door of the cabin.

"I say there, Gatlin, for christsake where are you?" He peers into the open door, blinking. "Reveal yourself. Break out the ice, man."

He holds a jug in his large, hairy, freckled hand, a quart of something potable clutched in a paper sack.

"Speak, O vocalissimus," he roars.

Gatlin comes out on the catwalk of the tower and looks down. Grins, says nothing, but at once begins to descend the stairway. Ballantine looks up, shading his eyes against the glare of the sun.

"Hey! You're up there. Get on down here. God damn it to hell, come down."

They sit at the old picnic table near the pump, beside the rusted horseshoe pegs and the chopping block. The bottle between them, a glass in Ballantine's hand, a tin cup before Gatlin. Canteen of branch water on the boards.

"Actually don't drink much of this stuff any more."

"I've noticed you're sipping rather daintily, man. For the love of God's bod, drink up. This is a great occasion."

"I am glad to see you again, Art."

"Glad? Rejoice! I've come to rescue you from exile. To drag you out of this Godforsaken wilderness. How much longer can you let yourself rot in this unspeakable, slovenly"—Ballantine waves his big hand at the surrounding and nearly silent forest—"this *blague* of nothingness?"

"I like it."

"You look good. But your mind is starving. For the sake of your nerves you're starving your mind and drying up your soul. You're becoming a spinster. Will Gatlin, our maiden aunt."

"It's nature."

"Fuck nature. Where we throw our empty beer cans on a Sunday afternoon. Man, get out of here before you die. If you live that long."

Neglecting the drink, Gatlin reloads his short evil pipe. Strikes a match on the tabletop.

Ballantine watches the steady hands. "Yes, you look well. But my God, Will, how many years at this now? Six? Seven?"

"Six."

"Six years in the primeval bog."

"Not all of it here. Various places."

Ballantine laughs. "Various places, he says. Christ, man, what kind of places? Some of them worse than this. That hellish sandtrap you were in two years ago. What did they call it? Death Valley? Good God, what a hole! Those others. And now this . . . a rotting forest. What do you do for women? Make love to your fist?"

He grins. "Whatever's handy."

"You're becoming a freak, Will. A fanatic. A weird queer kind of anchorite. You're dreaming your life away."

"Oh no, it's not that bad."

"Drink." Ballantine half fills his glass, adds water from Gatlin's canteen. "Not that bad, eh? You ever hear from the ex?"

"No. She doesn't write."

"The kid ever write you?"

"Yes."

"Thank God for that. Support payments?"

"I do what I can."

"Thank God for that too. I'd hate to see you escape scot-free, man, when all the rest of us are paying blood. Through the nose. Through the nose, Will. Visualize. O pussy-whipped men of America, visualize."

"I'm trying."

"But don't let her bleed you to death. The ex-wife is

like a succubus. The bitter half. The older they get the more bitter; they never forget and they never forgive. They'll bleed a man to death if they can. And then throw the empty shell into the garbage can and cash in his life insurance. And hang his picture upside down, face to the wall, behind the water heater. And sow salt on his grave. Adding salt to insult. Don't let her do that to you, Will. But you've got to make a fresh start. Get out of the woods here, shape up a bit, take a decent sort of job—you could always go back to teaching, you know, man, it pays better than ever now, they're screaming for instructors, assistant professors, yes and the girls are better than ever —and then, when you're set, find yourself a good strong simple-minded wench, like my new one, for example, Elsie I mean, and *hurl yourself upon her.* In fact you can have Elsie if you want her."

"She's a fine woman."

"She's a bitch." Ballantine drinks deep, lowers the glass. Wipes his broad mouth. "But a good one, mind, a good bitch. In her goddamned cockeyed way she loves me, I'll say that much for her. The kid has judgment. If only she weren't so ugly. One thing I cannot and will not suffer is an ugly woman. There's no excuse for it."

He thinks, *Dishonoring his wife, he dishonors himself. Spare us, old friend, these reductions.*

"Of course," Ballantine goes on, "I know what you're thinking. In the dark it's all the same, the standing cock hath no conscience, let alone the power of making aesthetic discriminations." He pauses, grins. "Maybe that's why I suffer from penis envy. My penis has more fun than I do."

He adds bourbon and water to his glass, offers the same to Gatlin. Who shakes his head. "Will, get out of this. Do you know the etymology of the word 'idiot'? No? What kind of philologist have we got here? Idiot: from the Greek *idiotes,* meaning a 'private' person, one who is alone. By extension, one who lives alone."

"I'm not alone."

"You're not?"

"I have excellent company."

Ballantine frowns. "Yourself, I suppose. Don't give me that Thoreauvian bullshit, man. Listen, leave this Smokey Bear stuff for the local jokels. They can hack it, they've got nothing to begin with anyway. But outside there's a world, Will. The great world. All yours. Full of fruit, wine, beautiful ideas, lovely and lascivious ladies, enchanted cities, gardens of electricity and light."

"I've been there."

"Hah! listen to the—"

"Well quit of all that."

"Ah, listen to the sonofabitch. He's been there before. Well quit of the world. Jesus. Jesus. Jesus X. Christ. Where have I heard all this crap before? Where haven't I heard it all before?"

Gatlin, patiently smoking his pipe, says nothing.

"Will, you need a woman."

He lifts one eyebrow.

"Yes, a woman. Sex."

"Love?"

"No, not love for godsake. Who said anything about love? Love is a disease. A social disease. A romantic, venereal, medieval disease. A hangover from the days of the fornicating troubadours and the gentlemen in iron britches. A disease for which marriage is the perfect cure. Never confuse love and sex. Fatal mistake."

"I do get them mixed up."

"Yes, you do. I'm sure you do. That's your trouble, man. So you've got to get out of here, get a job, a real job, a man's job—"

"Become a professor like you."

"That's it. And grab a woman. Help the movement. Liberate a woman tonight. You'll get stale out here in the woods, living like a bear. Your balls will shrink, your tongue grow stiff and heavy. Your mind will wither away. Whatever became of William Gatlin? Went mad flogging his bloody duff."

"Poor Willy."

"Poor Will, poor Will, poor Will, sick ghost of a dead bird haunting the woods of nowhere."

Sad, sad . . .

"Prematurely middle-aged. Evading life. Wasting away. Look at you, flat as a board, you don't get enough to eat for christsake. When's the last time you had a full dinner, served by the woman who loves you?"

"Art, you shake me."

"Just trying to wake you up, old buddy. Life is short."

"Life is long."

"Life is too short."

"Life is very long."

And now melancholy, like the shadow of a cloud, passes over them both. In the quiet forest.

The gaunt and hungry mule deer, Gatlin's parasites, stand in the shadows waiting for sundown. Ballantine's roving eyes seek them out, while his hands refill his glass.

"Your friends are here again. God, look at those scroungy brutes. Like gigantic . . . Yes, they remind me of gigantic stuffed rabbits."

"The deer? They're starving. Too many for the range."

"Feed them."

"They're spoiled enough already."

"Shoot them."

"I'll take a couple in the fall. They're no good now."

"So what's the solution?"

"We need more lions, wolves and coyotes."

Ballantine turns his back on the deer. "Outside we have plenty of wolves."

"Yes, I remember."

"Another reason why we need you, Will, out there. You've got no right to hide in here like a monk in a monastery. It's cowardly."

"No right? Well, I was sick of all the talk. The petitions and the protests. When the shooting starts I'll come out."

"Then it will be too late."

His pipe is dead, he's trying to smoke the bottom of the bowl. Sun sinking in a reef of clouds. Gatlin excuses himself, hurries up the tower for an evening look at things. Ballantine hauls his heavy bulk up from the bench, steps toward the edge of the clearing, unzips and pisses heartily on the fallen leaves, the dust, the pine needles. Zips and backs off. Some of the deer approach. Ballantine clambers slowly up the stairway. The tower shakes.

Joins Gatlin on the catwalk.

"Whew! Christ! Jesus, how many times a day you climb this goddamned thing?"

Gatlin peers into the northwest, shading his eyes. The binoculars hang by a strap from his neck.

Ballantine sags over the rail and stares down at the ground far below, where the deer are now moving slowly through the clearing, heads lowered, nuzzling the earth. Two of them circle the stain of Ballantine's urine, striking at each other; one retires. All does and fawns. Thin gray shapes, silent as shadows. Tiring of them, he looks where Gatlin is looking.

"What do you see?"

"Nothing."

"What are you looking at then?"

Gatlin does not answer.

"I don't see it," Ballantine says. He smiles to himself, hums a tune. "What happens to this tower when the wind blows hard?"

"It sways."

"And lightning? St. Elmo's fire?"

"Yes, there's some of that too."

"You're mad. You're a madman, Will. This place is driving you out of your mind. Let's go down to the lodge and have a big dinner."

"Stay here tonight. I was about to start supper."

"I know your suppers. Thanks anyway. And Elsie's waiting for me at the lodge. She'd love to see you. Come and eat with us. We have to get an early start tomorrow."

"Back to California?"

"Yes. Summer session begins in three days. They need me. They're calling."

"Stay here, both of you. Take a summer off."

Ballantine smiles. "Can't do it, man. Can't do it."

"You owe it to yourself, Art. I think you've earned it, Art."

"He mocks me. He jests at my burdens. Why don't *you* come with *us*?"

"I can't leave the job."

"Job? You call this a job? This Boy Scout stuff?"

"Someone's got to do it."

"So. But why you?"

He makes no reply. Ballantine waits. Tries again.

"Will?"

"Yeah?"

"Why are you here?"

No reply.

"What in God's name do you think you're doing here? What do you *really* want to do anyway?"

"Really want to do," Gatlin repeats softly, still gazing out over the forest. Toward the desert. A pause. "Stare at the sun," he says.

"What?"

"Stare it down."

Ballantine sighs. "Will, you're crazy."

"Stare it out," says Gatlin, smiling. "Stand on this tower and stare at the sun until the sun goes . . . black."

"Let's get out of here. You need a drink. No, I need a drink. We all need a drink. I'm sorry I asked."

They descend the tower. They walk down the darkening pathway. The deer watch, their mule ears alert; in silhouette they look like giant hares. Down the trail, under the breathing and whispering trees, through a grove of crooked aspen in a green-gold fading light. The hermit thrush. Two men walking beneath the glowing and heartbreaking sky, where mountainous clouds drift against the wheeling spokes of evening, toward the evening star. One talking.

His arm on Gatlin's shoulders, Ballantine speaks of love. A two-time loser, he speaks of marriage. A doctor of philosophy, he speaks of duty, honor, obligation and the world. He speaks of choice, of decision, of creation and significance. Of purpose and meaning. Of happiness. Of joy.

Gatlin swings his stick. He stops for a moment, pointing at something deep in the shadows among the trees.

"What?" Ballantine stares. "Yes? What is it, Will?"

Gatlin points.

"What do you see, Will?"

7

SAW HER smiling reflection rise beside his. The sunlight shone through her hair. He felt her hands move up his back, onto his shoulders, into his hair.

She started to laugh, and with the sudden strength that always surprised him she pushed his head down, into the water. And ran away, laughing, toward the aspen trees, through the silken knee-high green rice grass. Those slim brown legs, bare beneath the short kilt, flashing through the shining grass. Her long hair, gleaming like copper, streamed out behind her.

He pounded after her but she ran like a startled doe, quick with life, sprang over a log and was into the trees before he even began to gain on her. In the green gloom she raced before him, laughing. He yelled, she looked back, veered to one side, then the other. Each time she changed direction he crossed the angle of her course and closed the gap. She collapsed suddenly on the edge of another grassy place, a small and sunlit opening deep in the forest. He sprawled upon her.

"Got you now, rabbit."

"You got me."

"You run like a rabbit." His heart was beating furiously. "First like a doe. Then like a rabbit."

"Dirty old man."

"Aye, lass."

"Dirty filthy hairy old beast."

"Aye, lassie. Old enough."

His hand moved upon her and she shivered, turned, twisted beneath him. He kissed her long and deep, caressed her, gasped with pleasure when he found her naked beneath the kilt.

"You were expecting me."

"Yes. There."

He kissed her hair, her forehead, her darkened eyelids, closing the bright and expectant eyes. Raising his lips, he drew back for a moment and she gazed steadily up at him. In the green and gold and hazel of her eyes he saw a brief reflection of the trees, the sky.

" 'Your eyen two wol slee me sodenly . . .' "

"Chaucer wrote that."

"You're right, lass."

"What else do you know?"

" 'I may the beaute' of them not sustene.' "

"Slay me."

"Yes."

"Kiss me."

"Yes. Shut up and I'll kiss you."

He kissed her mouth, unbuttoned her blouse and stroked the small soft breasts, feeling the nipples rise and harden under his touch.

"Yes. There. Kiss me there."

He kissed them, nibbled on them. Her arms tightened fiercely around his neck. He touched her knees, the silken skin above. Her thighs parted slowly before his hand.

"Yes, oh Will. There, there . . ."

Her warm sex was soft and sleek as velvet when he slipped a finger into her.

"Oh Will. Please. Oh God. Oh Will, I want to say all the words."

"Say them."

"I don't know how."

"Say fuck."

"Fuck. Fuck me."

"Yes. Say cock. Say cunt."

"Cock. Cunt. Cock. Oh Will . . ."

"Say cocksucker."

"Cocksucker. Will. Oh God. Oh Jesus."
"Jesus? Jesus who?"
"Jesus H. Christ."
"Thatta girl. Say the words."
"Cock. Cunt. Fuck. Jesus H. Christ." She was turning, trembling, opening for him. "Oh God, Will. Now. Fuck me. Fuck me."
"Where?"
"Oh God. Please."
"Where?"
"In my. In my."
The sun sparkled through the shaking shimmering trim translucent leaves. The warm grass surrounded them, bedded them, embraced them. An orange-black butterfly danced in the air, in the light. Monarch of the moment.

Dear heart how like you this

8

LATE IN THE MORNING he descends from the tower. Enters the cabin, stokes up the fire, reheats his coffee. Afterwards, tamping down the tobacco in the bowl of the pipe, he walks to the little outhouse down the slope, away from the cabin and the trail. Passing on the way the red-painted firebox where the tools are stored—sharpened spades, axes, mattock, Pulaski, portable water pump—and his emergency pack, the hard hat, the C rations.

Entering the outhouse, leaving the door wide open, facing the white aspens and the darker trees beyond, he lowers his trousers and sits. Lights the pipe. This ceremony too he enjoys as much almost as any other. The order, the decorum, the satisfaction of completeness. All excretions, he recalls, are pleasurable. The inside of the little pine house is clean and austere, smelling faintly of lime and the whitewash on the inside walls. On the floor is a bucket filled with ashes, the gray wood ashes from the cabin stove; he will pour some of the ashes into the pit before he leaves, to keep the flies down, the office pure and sweet. The man has a quiet passion for method and exactness, at least here, in this.

He smokes, gazing out at the forest.

All is silent. The sky low, heavy, a gray still overcast. One bird swoops down and across among the trees but disappears, making no sound.

Returning to the cabin, buckling his belt, he is halted by a soft voice
>   *Will*
>   calling his name.

He stops, looks back and around, searches the depths of the forest. But there is nothing. He sees only what is there, the living and dying trees, the flowers of red and purple penstemon crowding the trunk of a fallen pine, the dim form farther back of a single yearling doe, its head up and alert, facing him. Listening.

He listens.

9

BALLANTINE PARKS his automobile in front of a tourist cabin near the lodge. He looks at Gatlin.

"Say, would you mind waiting in the car a minute?" He grins, a little embarrassed. "She might not be . . . well, ready for us."

Waiting, he hears the voices coming from inside the

cabin, Ballantine's voice and a woman's voice, Elsie's voice. She sounds irritable, exasperated, and her tone sharpens as Ballantine tries to mollify her. Gatlin tries not to hear the words. The conversation or rather the argument seems to grow more intense. Bastard. He hears the word called bastard. Repeatedly. Clearly.

Ballantine looms bearlike in the open doorway, a red scowl of anger on his face. The door slams shut with a crash as he approaches the car. He gets in, backs off, racing the engine, shifts into low and jumps the clutch. With a screech of rubber, like schoolboys, they lunge into the road. For once Ballantine says nothing. Gatlin has nothing to say. They park again one block away in front of the lodge. For a minute, two minutes, they sit in the car and look at the people going into the building and the people coming out of the building.

"Elsie's not having dinner with us." Ballantine waits for a comment from his friend.

"Sorry."

"Sorry, is that all you can say, sorry? I told you she was a bitch."

"Sorry. It's a bitch."

Ballantine grins, slaps Gatlin's knee. "Fuck her. Fuck her, I say, god damn it, with all due consideration." He stares at the young girls going into the lodge; leaving the lodge. College girls, high school girls, in miniskirts and fantastic stockings, in skin-tight pants with brave vibrating heart-shaped bottoms. "Lord, look at that, Will. Look at them. Look at them. Look at them. The treasures of this earth. Behinds like valentines."

A pause. Gatlin is silent.

"Look at that." Ballantine groans. "All that fresh sweet succulent young cunt. My God, Will, they've got us outnumbered twenty to one.

"You can't have them all."

"I don't want them all. I just want all the ones I want. Will, I could eat that stuff with a spoon."

A pause. Gatlin says nothing.

"If only I had a spoon. I want it so bad I can taste it. Don't you ever hunger for the bearded oyster? The hairy clam?"

"Let's go in."

"Naw, you wouldn't even remember what it looks like."

"Let's go in, Art."

Inside, in the dining room, at a table with candle and white linen, Ballantine orders two martinis. Doubles. He stares after the retreating cocktail waitress.

"She said her name is Sheila."

Now the table waitress comes up, pencil and pad in hand. Young, too young, she has golden Mormon hair, blueberry eyes, a round and rosy, sweet, ingenuous face. For a girl so young her breasts are very large. Ballantine begins again.

"What's your name, young lady?"

"Kathy."

"You are beautiful, Kathy."

The girl blushes; her smile grows wider. She is beautiful. They are all beautiful.

"My name is Art," says Ballantine. "Artless Art. Where are you from, Kathy?"

"Bountiful."

"How true. How unquestionably true. And where is that, Miss Kathy?"

"Bountiful, Utah."

"Thank you, Miss Kathy. And now, young lady, we are ready to order."

When she leaves he says to Gatlin, "Why are all girls named Kathy these days?"

"They're not."

"Haven't you noticed? Kathy or Sheila, all of them."

"They're not."

"It's really curious." He beckons again to the cocktail waitress. "Sheila," he says. She comes forward. "See what I mean," he says to Gatlin. "Have another? No?"

After the dinner they have coffee and cognac and then go to the bar, where Ballantine orders more cognac.

"Sheep," he says, beginning to maunder. "I hate them. I hate sheep. Did you ever look a sheep in the eye, Will? Slots. Look a sheep in the eye and all you see is a cold black. slot. On a yellow eyeball. No soul, Will. Like women. No soul."

"You seem to like lamb."

"Do not mock. Will, I'm drunk, I believe, but I'm still entitled to have my say, am I not? Will, I say she hates me. She has no soul. Do not mock me."

In the corner of the bar sit three Indian men, Hopis, with a pair of lady tourists in their midst, on their hands. Two of the Indians are drunk and the third is unconscious. Gatlin knows them but tonight he does not know them, he keeps his back turned. Good men but bad medicine on a night like this. One sick Indian on his hands already.

"She's going to leave me, Will."

"No she's not."

"I hate to sound maudlin, old meatball, but she's going to leave me. Eyes like slots."

"Not over one little fight."

"Will, this has been going on for months. She hates me, and you know why she hates me?"

Gatlin is silent.

"Because I am unfaithful, Will. Will, I am going to tell you the truth. I screw students."

"Most professors do that."

"Girl students."

"What else?"

"I even bring them home at night. Female types mostly.

That's what makes Elsie so mad. She goes into the bathroom in the morning and there's some mysterious stranger squatting on the toilet bowl, tinkling contentedly, with Elsie's douche bag in her hands."

"That's going too far."

"Will, I've got this problem. Will, there's something wrong with me. All I can ever think about is cunt." He pauses, then speaks in a dramatic whisper: *"It's like an obsession."*

"Let's go home now, Art. She'll let you in now."

"The clitoris, Will, the clitoris. There's the key. The key to a woman's heart. And that's Greek too."

He helps him to his feet. "Come on."

The Hopis watch, grinning, unable to rise, their eyes the complexion of sun-ripened strawberries. "Hey, Will," they call, "what yah got there?"

"Who's that?" Ballantine blinks and levels his formidable stare at the Indians and their two ladies.

"Friends of mine from Polacca. Let's go."

"Will," they call.

Ballantine turns away, grumbling, and takes a reading on the door. "Let's get out of here," he says. "Goddamn zoo. It's like a zoo, Will. Men, women, monkeys. All they ever think about is sex. It's disgusting. Because they're in this cage, don't you see? Pardon me, sir."

Through the door and out into the sweet wet forest air. Together they descend the steps toward Ballantine's car, stumbling once as Ballantine misses a riser. Into the car.

"Because it's like a cage. There's nothing else for them to do. Will, we got to tear this cage apart someday. Turn it upside down and inside out."

A light rain is falling now. He drives Ballantine back to his rented cabin and his wife.

"Maybe I should lay off the booze, Will. Maybe I should go back to dope. The old giggleweed." He pauses.

"No, I guess I'll stick to booze. Every man has to be good at something. I'll become a great drunkard."

"You're drunk." He stops and shuts off the motor.

"A good gray wise old juicehead, that's what I'll be. With a purple carbuncular nose. Hell, Will, any punk kid can get high on grass. It takes a man to handle liquor."

"You're home now, Art."

"A man. Okay, home. Cabin number forty-two, yeah. Elsie Ballantine lives here, bless her. The liberated woman. Come on in, we'll make a sandwich."

No answer from Gatlin.

"What do you say? Ham sandwich? Sexual sandwich? Soda pop?"

"Thanks, no."

"It's all right, she'll be asleep now."

"No thanks, I'd rather not."

"Will, how can you live like this?"

"What do you mean?"

"Alone. Alone. How can you live this way? It's inhuman. You're murdering yourself." Ballantine waits. "All right, don't say anything. But it's true and you know it."

They sit there in the dark, in the car, staring at the rainy windshield. "I say this because I love you, you know."

"I know, Art."

The soft and midnight rain. "God damn it, Will, say something." He waits. "Will you say something?"

Waiting. "Anything?"

The rain falls quietly on the car, on the grass and the cabin, on the tall dark pines in the night, on the forest to the north and west, and beyond the rim, into that abyss which divides the plateau.

10

HER PLACE. A small white wooden house, not far from the clinic. The house divided into two apartments; she lived in the one next to the forest. There were four rooms, all of them bright and sunny during the day—the kitchen, with its refrigerator, gas stove, sink and cabinets, counter, broom closet, ironing board, two chairs, the small white table with folding leaves, on which she always kept a pair of wine bottles, one of them overlaid with candle wax in many colors, the other containing water and a few flowers, always; the large room in front, her living room, with sofa, chairs, desk, a phonograph and records (Coltrane, Coleman and Davis, Dylan and Baez, the Beatles, the Supremes, the Stones, others, and Chopin, Debussy, Mahler, Ravel, Tchaikowsky, Puccini), a bookcase holding her schoolgirl books (Golding and Salinger and Tolkien and *War and Peace* and *Winnie the Pooh*), her collapsible easel and water-color set, her old bleached immaculate horse's skull on the wall, her posters, her driftwood fragments, her dead juniper limb, her tiny Navajo rug; the bathroom with more candles in wine bottles for bathing by candlelight, and pink Kleenex and flowered toilet paper, and sculptured cakes of soap, and the very long, very deep old-fashioned tub, and the floral-decorated mirror on the door of the little cabinet where she kept her aspirins and the b.c. pills in their calibrated dispenser, the toothpaste and deodorant and hand lotion and shampoo, and on the wall photographs in color of lonely deep-sea fish; and the bedroom: a small bed covered by an Indian blanket, a chair, a chest of drawers, a wardrobe closet, her trunk and empty luggage, and the vanity table on which lay her brush and comb, her eyebrow pencil, her tube of fluid eye shadow, a tin of talcum powder, a vial of perfume, a letter.

11

HE WAS ADDRESSING an envelope when someone touched him gently on the elbow. "Mr. Gatlin."

A girl stood beside him, slim and brown, smiling. The long hair framed her sunburned face, the clear gray-green steady eyes. "Hello." At first he couldn't remember her. "Sandy?"

"Well, I'm glad you at least remember my name. You looked kind of uncertain."

She wore what was called a minidress, a thin flimsy thing in psychedelic yellow, which left her arms bare to the shoulder, and the fine legs exposed high above the knee. She wore no makeup or jewelry, the small front teeth revealed by the smile appeared to be just a trace crooked, and her nose was peeling. He wasn't sure whether she was pretty or not; he decided that she was.

"Your nose is peeling."

"Thanks."

"I meant that as a compliment."

"Thanks a lot. Well I earned it. I crossed the canyon yesterday, all the way, rim to rim."

"That's a good walk." He hesitated. "How's your friend the rodeo queen?"

"You mean Gloria? She quit two weeks ago. Not enough excitement around here for her. I did it all by myself."

"Did what all by yourself?"

"Hiked the canyon. Want to buy me a Coke?"

"What? Sure. You really hiked it alone?"

"Yes sir. Not all in one day, of course. I spent a night down by the river."

Gatlin was impressed. "That can be dangerous. Never go alone."

"Oh I stayed on the trail all the way. What could happen? It was great. Buy me a Coke?"

"For that I'll buy you a drink. If you promise never to do it again. Here, let me get rid of this." Gatlin mailed his letter. They went outside, into the blazing sunshine, and walked toward the lodge. "What do you do here?"

"I'm working at the clinic as a nurse's aid. I told you that before. You don't come down here very often, do you? I saw you in the post office and I thought, Well, if you want to say hello to him you'd better do it now, you might never get another chance. And the first thing you mention is my peeling nose."

"You have a very nice nose and I'm glad you saw me." He led her toward the door of the bar.

She stopped. "I can't go in there."

"Why not?"

"I'm nineteen, Mr. Gatlin."

He looked at her again. "Of course." My God, he thought, there's an entire new generation pursuing us now. "Okay. Let's get that Coke. And you don't have to call me Mr. Gatlin. Call me Will."

She smiled up at him. "Yes sir." Her eyes were bright, green, golden, amused; their color seemed to change with every change from shadow to light. "How old are you, Mr. Gatlin?"

"Thirty-seven."

"Really? Why you're old enough—"

"To be your mother. Yes."

"You don't look it."

"I'm very well preserved for my age."

Over her Coke and his coffee she studied his face. "I like those wrinkles around your eyes. You have a rugged old grizzled look."

"Drink your Coke."

"Are you part Indian?"

"Are you part dryad?" He looked carefully at this fresh wench sitting before him, only the table between them. Was she teasing him? She seemed to be serious now, yet he thought he still saw the mocking glint of play in her eyes. He felt the first hint of boredom in this meeting; he thought of the students, he thought of the classroom he had walked out of, for good, six years before.

"What's a dryad?"

"A kind of wood nymph."

"No, I'm Scotch, mostly."

"Scotch is a whiskey." He realized now that the girl, though she concealed it well, was actually nervous. "What's your last name?"

"MacKenzie. Sandra MacKenzie. I told you that before. Ridiculous name, isn't it? You don't remember things, do you, Mr. Gatlin?"

"I remember far too much." That'll sock her, he thought.

"Ooooh." Her eyes widened. "How dramatic. How sad. That's a cool thing to say. But it's true, isn't it? I can tell." She was examining his face again, trying to read him. "Yes, you do have a rather sad-looking face. But it's a good face. You have . . . kind eyes."

"Kind of you to say that."

"But so dark. And all that black hair. And that big nose. I'll bet you are part Indian."

He smiled.

She smiled at him, freely, warmly, exposing those slightly crooked but clear almost translucent front teeth.

43

She did not smile easily or often, despite the brightness in her manner. She was, he saw, really a shy and anxious little girl. Ah yes . . . they grow up slow in this country. And the boys are slower than the girls. And the parents even slower than the children. And slowest of all, he thought, are the aging adolescents, the degenerate old dogs like Arthur Ballantine. And William C. Gatlin. Those atavists from the time of Ethelred. The Unready.

When he said nothing more she lowered her head and sucked up the last of her drink through the straw; the flaked ice rattled noisily in the bottom of the glass. He watched the light glistening in the deep copper-colored masses of her hair. She raised her head and faced him squarely.

"Well," she said. "What now?" She waited for him to reply. He didn't. "Would you like . . ." But she hesitated.

"I ought to go home, Sandy."

"Home? Now?"

"Back to the lookout. Fix my bachelor supper." What he actually had in mind, however, first, was a drink or two with his Polacca Hopi friends in the bar. After that a visit to the store for another week's supplies, and then the trip back into the forest.

Her smile had faded away, some of the brightness left her eyes. She gazed at him with an unconsciously lost, appealing expression which he recognized, reluctantly, as being exactly what it appeared to be: an appeal. The damned child was lonely. What's wrong here? The boy friend leave her? Surely she had one.

Both tried to speak at once.

"Why . . ."

"I could . . ." Again she stopped. "Excuse me."

"Go ahead."

"Well, I was going to say. I mean, I am a pretty good

cook, Mr. Gatlin. I'm very good at stuffed peppers. Yes, I am. Do you like stuffed peppers?"

They stared at each other in silence for a prolonged moment, amazed by something wild and strange and sweet which seemed to have come suddenly into the space which both separated and united them. By the slow rising motion of motes of golden dust floating in the shaft of light, long and slanting, which streamed through the window and across their table, across his coffee cup and her empty glass, across their hands.

Slowly, Sandy began to smile again. And Gatlin smiled. Her smile broadened, brightened. They started to laugh.

"Peppers," he said, in awe and wonder, mimicking the girl. "Stuffed peppers. I'm very good at stuffed peppers, Mr. Gatlin. Oh yes I am." And they leaned to one another, joined in laughter.

While she stuffed her peppers he worked on the cork of the bottle of wine he had bought. The cork was rotten and Sandy's corkscrew too small. He finally popped the cork by tapping on the bottom of the bottle with a block of wood. She set two tall-stemmed glasses on the table. He poured a little wine into one glass, raised it to his nose and moved it slowly back and forth. *"Quel bouquet . . ."* She watched him, smiling. He sipped the wine, tasted, pursed his lips, narrowed his eyes and nodded to an invisible attendant at his side. *"C'est bien.* Very good, *garçon.* You may go." He filled her glass and his own. They raised their glasses, facing each other. "Remember," he said, "you must look into my eyes."

She put records on the phonograph. The music swirled around them like a cloud of stereophonic fire. That old man from Moscow, he thought, that beautiful old white-bearded queer in his lonesome dacha out in the forest. Aspens? Birches? She showed him her horse skull and her watercolors. Her Navajo rug. Her dead juniper branch, her posters and her driftwood. He admired them all. They waltzed with Tchaikowski. Halted.

"The peppers, MacKenzie, the peppers!"

She ran to the kitchen, opened the oven. "They're all right." With a towel she removed the baking dish, set it to cool for a minute on the lowered oven door. He peeled and sliced a cucumber into the salad, added more tomato, a sliced carrot and chunks of celery. She lit the candles on the table, in their old wax-encrusted wine bottles. They set the table. He refilled the glasses: the red wine glowed like music in the soft radiance of the burning candles. They sat facing each other, amazed by everything. "Bread?"

He broke a section from the loaf she offered him, watching her as he did it. Her bright eyes shining with delight, her small oval face as radiant as the wine. "Miss MacKenzie," he said. "Sandy," he said.

Gradually, course by course, she told him the story of her life. Of a childhood in Maryland and Virginia, her father an official in Washington.

"The boss," he said. "You're a spy for the boss."

"No, I'm a secret agent for the Sierra Club."

A prep school in Silver Springs. One year at Goucher College. Three months in Puerto Rico as a trainee with the Peace Corps.

"Peace Corps!"

"Don't laugh. It's no more ridiculous than what you're doing, sitting up in that treehouse all day like some kind of . . . ridiculous old owl."

"I think."

"On government time? They'll fire you."

What was she supposed to be doing in the Peace Corps? The Peace Corps was training her for a job in Peru or

Ecuador, where she was intended to show the native Indian ladies how to have and care for babies, how to cook, how to raise their children properly.

"You are kidding."

"Oh no. They were serious. Terribly serious. It was very sad."

"Is that why you quit?"

Here she became a little hesitant. "Partly that. And there was this boy I met. He . . ." She paused.

"Dark outside," Gatlin said. "I ought to be getting back to my treehouse. Have to go back to work tomorrow."

"Oh wait. Don't go yet."

"Shall we finish the wine?"

"Let's."

He emptied the bottle into their glasses. "Here's to the Peace Corps."

"To the Peace Corps." They drank.

"And the Boy Scouts of America."

"And the Girl Scouts of America." They drank again.

"Be prepared."

"I'm not. I think I'm getting smashed."

"And good old Big Nobodaddy up there watching over us. Watching over everybody. Watching over the whole wide world."

"Yes. Him too. I am. I am getting smashed."

They stopped, each a little tipsy, watching each other. Waiting. Now what? he thought. Shall I put her to bed? She looks ready enough. Willing enough. Lonely enough. Yes, he thought, the kid's in love. But not with me. He pushed back his chair, stood up.

"I'll put some more records on," she said.

"I'm going."

"Oh please. Not already."

"You're a sweet girl, Sandy. And it was a lovely dinner, for which I thank you."

"Please don't go yet."

She's waiting for a letter, he thought. And it doesn't come. I'll bet she's still a virgin. Nineteen years old, for godsake. Absurd. "Thank you very much," he said, "but I'd better get started. I'll see you again."

They walked together into the front room, toward the door. "I have to fly over to the other rim soon," she said, "to get my car. Could you come with me?"

"Give me a couple of days' notice."

"We'll have a picnic. I'll make a picnic basket and bring my sketchbook. We can go swimming in the river."

"Yes."

He opened the door. She came very close to him, almost touching, and looked up at him, into his eyes.

"Mr. Gatlin?"

"My name is Will."

"Oh. Will. Well, would you . . ."

"Yes?"

"Would you like to kiss me, Mr. Gatlin?"

"Very much."

"Then do it."

And she closed her eyes. He kissed her, lightly, on the small soft mouth. Her arms came up and closed about his neck and held him. He kissed her again, better this time, and felt her lips part hungrily beneath his. After a while he drew back and gently disengaged her arms. She sighed and rested her head against his chest.

"Mr. Gatlin," she said.

"Call me Will."

"Will," she said, "do you think I'm . . ."

"Yes. You are beautiful. You are a very beautiful girl, Sandy."

Now she raised her head and looked up at him again, tears of pleasure in her eyes. "Oh. Yes. Oh, nobody's told me that for months!"

12   Dear Willy,

Well, compañero, qué pasa? Let me give you my great tidings first—she left me, my Elsie, my sweet and irreplaceable Elsie with her great white ass and her hairy armpits and all the rest. Gave me the slip on the sly, she did, walking out while I was away. Can't say I blame her one bit, of course. Back to the homefolks, Gawd help her. Anything to get away from Ballantine.

But never mind. My irreplaceable Elsie has already been replaced. Yes. Her name is Darnelle, she's only 29, she has brown eyes, secondary mammaries and—all the rest. Do not misunderstand me, I am not going to marry the woman. We have agreed to share my humble penthouse for a time, on a trial basis, you see, endeavoring in that way to lay the foundations of a durable union. But marry the woman? I should say not. Why spoil a perfectly good relationship? Why buy a cow when I can get all the milk I need through the fence?

They murmur of love. Live for love, they whine in my ear; live for the fulfillment which only love can bring, they whimper in their term papers. What do they mean, fulfillment? What is a man, some kind of a jug, that he has to be fulfilled? And this continual hysterical bleating for love, for love, for love, like a herd of goddamned sheep for christsake! Baaa . . . baaa . . . baaa. I say—and listen carefully, friend Gatlin—I say, give us some wolves. Man, in this sick sheepfold, give us some wolves.

Love? I love *women,* god damn it. I guess I'm queer, Will: I love *women.* Not this one or that one but all of them, god damn it, all of them. Even me old mother, bless her saintly gash.

I tell you, Will old buzzard, in your lonely forest roost, I tell you, marriage is a dying institution in our society. That's why it smells so bad. And you know why it's dying? I'll tell you, Will old comrade. No one else will tell you but I will tell you. Marriage in our society is rotting away from too much love. They're killing it with love. Romantic love. They marry for love, the bloody fools, turn their backs on the world and start sucking each other's blood. They poison marriage with love. They feed on each other, they cling to each other, all these lonely desperate couples all over America cut off from the earth, cut off from the past, cut off from any sense of a common life, just these miserably lonely, frightened couples with their miserably lonely, frightened brats, all feeding on one another like parasites, each man demanding from his wife what no single isolated woman could possibly give or be, each woman demanding from her husband the strength and security and tenderness which is beyond the power of any single isolated man. Because they have nothing else they bank all their hopes on marriage and inevitably they are disappointed. Love and marriage cannot give anyone more than a token of what we all need. Love and marriage in themselves are not enough. And so in disappointment they turn against each other, these stranded and lonely couples, and their love soon sours into hate.

Well, old buddy, we know all about this, eh? We've been through this mill, eh comrade? And so I say—but what shall I say? I have no answer. Not yet, anyway. But

I'm working on it. I'll give you a solution one of these days.

Enough of all that rubbish. What are you doing? Come down out of your tower and give us the word. Come to California. We need you here. My God, Will, you must see it, the glossy living wenchery that surrounds me on all sides, these flashy coeds, these well-fleshed females, these flashy fleshy fillies with their filigreed eyelids and callipygian fannies. The ingenious depravities these tender creatures are capable of. Shocking, I say, even to a hardened Christian like myself. But are you tempted? No, not you, up there in your tower, happily beating away in solitary satisfaction on the old family tom-tom. But I must warn you, Willy, there's a limit to what flesh and blood may endure. You'll go blind. You'll go insane. Your hair will fall out and your palms grow hairy. You know all that.

A riddle, Willy:
What is both desperate and absurd?

I had a dream the other day. A daydream. I saw the earth, our great planet of basalt, granite and iron, as a kind of spherical altar on which we sacrifice, generation after generation, for a million and one years, the lives of all humanity. And this terrible ball was draped with blood, like a Sherwin-Williams paint ad. We cover the earth. Draped with blood and soaked with tears.

And what keeps it all going? We know, don't we, compadre? We know. That guilty stealth of lovers, as they sneak into the dark behind the bushes to do their dirty work. And the post coitum tristus, eh? But who can fight it, man?

A poem, Willy, for you:

> Breathes there the man with balls so dead
> Who never to himself hath said,

"You know, by christ, come to think of it,
I could use some strange ass in *my* bed."

Well, just a thought.

So write, you bastard. You owe me three letters. Four now. At least a picture postcard maybe? You and a sunset canyon scene, with one drunk Hopi in foreground and the sky beyond all lushed up in gorgeous reds and yellows like one of Gawd's own celestial pizza pies.

The Lyf so short, the Art so hard to lerne.

—Art (Ph.D.)

13

EACH AFTERNOON resembles every other afternoon now, in early summer, before the season of the lightning. Across that transparent sea of blue drift a few small clouds, isles of vapor with clean hard edges, forming out of nothing, apparently, at an immense altitude, reshaping themselves as they float slowly eastward with the prevailing wind, all in uniform motion and direction like a fleet of ships, coalescing with one another, dissipating, vanishing as they came, into nothing. The sky remains, a hot black-grained mirror of nothing, unchanged by their passage.

Walking the catwalk around and around, like a prisoner in solitary (but a prisoner who no longer even dreams of freedom, a prisoner so long imprisoned in his life that he can no longer distinguish between liberty and confinement, between his present state and any possible other), he sees . . . what does he see? Nothing to report. Nowhere, at any point, that pillar of smoke. That signal.

Only the trees, the breathing forest, the far-off forms of rising mountains, the remote desert. And bending across the plateau the white wall of the canyon's farther rim, glaring in the sunlight, miles away. From the depths of the canyon, which he cannot see from the tower, there comes, each day at this time, the same faintly purple mist of shadow, a hint of the darkness of the inner gorge, like a premonition of twilight.

He is not in the least oppressed by the slow advance of the minutes, the hours, the day. There seems to him to be no difference of any importance between his time and that of any other he has known, between his time and that of the living and decaying trees below his platform, between his time and the transformations of the rock on the canyon's rim.

Now it is midafternoon.

Now it is sundown.

14

In the bar with Hugh Sequinsky, Chief Anthony and Roberto.

"I can speak French too," says Hugh.

"*Parlez anglais, s'il vous plaît.*"

"No, I want to speak French."

"Let him talk French," Chief Anthony says. "He's very good at it."

"I spent two years over there," Hugh explains. "I was a sergeant. What were you?"

"I was a sergeant too. Speak Hopi. I want to learn some Hopi."

"No, Hopi is too difficult for forest rangers. Maybe I

could teach you some Navajo, that's an easy language. Even kids can talk Navajo."

"Hopi kids."

"Maybe we ought to wake up Roberto and get the hell out of here before they throw us out."

"Drink up first."

"One more round, Gatlinsky."

"No, no more for me. I'm a workingman. I'm not an Indian."

"That's the trouble with you white men. You're not Indians."

"We have enough troubles already. Why do you Indians drink so much? Look at Roberto. I've never seen him sober yet. I've never even seen him when he wasn't already passed out. If you Indians are better than white men why do you drink so much?"

"Because we're Indians."

"Because?"

"Because we are very happy that we are not white men."

"Sorry, I can't accept that statement."

"All right, because watching you white men makes us so very unhappy we have to drink to forget your troubles."

"Not good enough."

"Come to Polacca, we'll explain everything. We'll fix you up."

"Be a Hopi?"

"Yes, be a happy Hopi. Be a happy Hopi hippie."

"Are Hopis really happier than anyone else?"

"We were."

"Are you really sure of that?"

"We were hippier anyway."

"We'll fix you up. We'll fix you up with a woman."

"A woman?"

"My sister. I sell you my sister for a new pickup; or I sell you my old pickup: GMC V-Eight, half ton with heavy duty clutch."

"Your sister has a heavy duty clutch?"

"You can bet your life."

"I'll try that."

"She has overdrive. She has four speeds forward. She has automatic transmission and coil springs. She has positive traction and independent suspension."

"Sounds like quite a girl."

"She's all woman."

"Quite a woman. Why don't you Indians get organized? If you Indians ever got organized you could take over the country."

"We don't want it now."

"You white men can keep it."

"We'll give it back to you."

"Keep it."

"Thanks."

"Thank you."

"There's only one thing I still don't understand about you Indians."

"What's that?"

"Twenty thousand years ago, during the Pleistocene, you killed off all the mastodons, camels, tree sloths, coryphodons and smilodons in America. Why?"

"Why?"

"Why?"

"Chief Anthony, would you care to answer the question? Why did we do that?"

"Why did we do that? I don't know. Ask Roberto."

"He's sleeping."

"Wake him up."

"Hugh, you're the intellectual. Why don't you answer the question?"

"I ain't no intellectual."
"You speak French, don't you?"
"*Mais oui. Je vous adore, mademoiselle.*"
"Then answer the question."
"We were hungry. *Voulez-vous—*?"
"Twenty thousand years ago you were hungry?"
"Yes."
"And now?"
"We're still hungry."
"Everybody's hungry. The deer are hungry. The mice are hungry. The wolves are hungry."
"The moon is hungry."
"The sun is hungry. Everybody."
"What will become of us?"
"The sun will eat the earth."
"No."
"Why not?"
"Because we shall eat the sun."
"You white men. You'll eat anything."
"We're hungry."
"You white men."
"You Indians."
"Let's have one more drink, Gatlinsky. One more and then we all go home. One for the trail. One more drink for that sad song in my heart. One for Chief Anthony. One for Roberto. One for me. One for you, Gatlinsky."

PART II
In the Sun

15

EARLY THAT MORNING he drove to the village, found the coffee shop open, breakfasted alone, spent ten minutes in the men's room (somewhat to his own surprise) recombing his shaggy black hair, which was too long, and brushing his teeth. When was the last time he had done this sort of thing, for a girl? Could hardly remember. A long time.

Seven-thirty by the coffee shop clock. He walked to her house.

She came out to meet him. "I saw you coming. I was afraid you might not come." The shy smile in the rosy lovely face. Her rich long burning hair, the bright eyes. To Gatlin she looked lovely. She was lovely. "I'm all ready," she added, lifting a rucksack from the porch steps.

"What's that?"

"This is our picnic. With wine and everything."

"You could've let me buy the wine."

"Don't get mad."

"Damn it, Sandy."

"What?"

"You are beautiful this morning."

"So are you." She touched his face with her hand. "So slick and smooth. You shaved with that straight razor, didn't you? And a clean shirt. All for me?"

"I even took a bath, lassie."

"Whether you needed it or not."

He took the rucksack. "Well, I'm not sure whether I needed it or not because I couldn't remember when I took the last one. This is heavy, what've you got in here?"

"You'll see. All kinds of goodies."

They walked through the trees toward the coffee shop and his truck. A gray squirrel scampered before them, raced up the trunk of a pine. Columns of light from the morning sun, blue with smoke from a hundred tourists' campfires, slanted across their path. A bus rumbled by loaded with schoolgirls on vacation.

She was wearing again that plaid kilt in which he had first seen her. "Flaunting the old tartan again, Mac-Kenzie?"

"Why not?" she said.

"Snobbery."

"Well why not? It's good to belong to something."

"That's what the gauleiter told the Hitler Youth."

"You're just jealous because you're just another ordinary mongrel American."

"My ancestors fought in the Revolution."

She laughed. "But on which side?"

"Aye, lass, that's the trouble. Some of them wore red coats and some wore red skins."

"Gatlin sounds like a hillbilly name."

"It is, it is."

"We knew your type back in Virginia. Naturally we didn't mix, socially. But they were allowed to vote, if they paid their poll tax."

"Democracy is wonderful. And what do you wear under it?"

"Wouldn't you like to know. None of your business. My but you're fresh this morning."

He put his arm around her small warm waist.

"It's a fresh morning, Sandy." He stopped her for a moment, kissed her on the side of the neck, on the lobe of her ear. Eyes wide, smiling, she stared past him at the sky.

"We'd better go," she said, "we'll miss that plane."

Oh stay, thou art so fair. "They'll wait," he said. Dropping the rucksack, embracing her, he kissed her long and hard on the mouth.

"We'd better go."

"This way."

He opened the door of the old truck for her. She climbed in and swung her long brown legs forward, modestly tugging at the short skirt.

"Don't look."

"You're beautiful."

"Well I'm glad someone thinks so."

"Shall I compare thee to a summer's day?"

"You're full of poetry this morning."

"Yes. My God, yes."

"God? Let's change the subject. Is there a God, Mr. Gatlin?"

He grinned at her and put his hand on her bare knee. "Is there an angry unicorn on the dark side of the moon? That's my answer to that question."

"You're clever but not very serious." She removed his hand. "Hadn't we better go?"

Driving toward the airport, he sang a song for her:

> "Eyes like the morning star,
> Lips like a rose,
> Sandy she's a pretty girl,
> God almighty knows.

"Will, there's something I should tell you."

Don't, he thought. I know it already. And he sang his other song for her:

> "O the boys of the column were waiting
> With hand grenades primed on the spot
> And the Irish Republican Army
> Made muck of the whole mucking lot."

"I'm engaged."

You're engaged. "That's nothing," he said. "I'm divorced."

"I guessed that."

"Where's your ring?"

"Well I'm not sure right now whether I'm engaged or not. He took the ring back for a while. But he still wants to marry me. I think."

"Who's he?"

"Larry Turner. Lawrence J. Turner the Third. He's a cadet in the Air Force. He's the boy I met in the Peace Corps. He's in love with me. I think."

"Okay."

"You're not angry, are you?"

He reached out and pulled her close, sinking his cheek in her silky, fragrant hair, watching the road with one eye, steering with one hand. "I wish you luck," he said. "And happiness too, what the hell."

"I don't know. Is happiness possible?"

"Anything is possible. You'll see."

"You're not angry with me?"

Disappointed, she means. "No, lass, why should I be? Is he a good man?"

"He's only twenty-three. But he's very serious about things."

Gatlin said nothing, while the wind roared past the open windows of the truck.

"I wish I had met you a year ago," the girl said.

"So do I," he agreed. "Better yet, ten years ago."

"Ten years ago I was nine years old."

"Even better."

"You are a dirty old man."

"You bet."

They pulled into the small private airport. As Gatlin had predicted, knowing what to expect, their pilot was still waiting for them, standing by his little Cessna talking with the only other passenger, a tall red-nosed bearded man with hiking gear on his back. Gatlin and Sandy paid their fares and climbed into the rear seats, the pilot got in, the hiker got in beside him, the pilot reached across and closed and secured the door. In five minutes they were all airborne and moving at what seemed like a tediously slow speed, almost stationary, far above the forested plateau.

"I think I could fly this thing myself," she said in his ear.

"Please don't try." Gatlin did not like airplanes; he knew they fell down, and as a mode of travel this kind of flight seemed to him too abstract, too removed from the earth. He could see nothing below but geography.

"I've had lessons," she said. "Fifteen hours. I've done everything except solo."

"You're an amazing kid."

"I'm going to hit the pilot on the head and take over."

"Okay. But not yet."

The plane hung suspended in the air, buzzing and vibrating like a huge fly, mechanical and incongruous, getting nowhere, while the edge of the canyon slipped past below and the world dropped down, down, down to the river's silver thread. The cliffs and towers rose vaguely out of the depths, pink and purple in the morning light, half obscured by haze. On some of those island buttes no man, white or red, had ever stood. Land of zoological legend, he thought. Of the trilobite, the crinoid, and the three-toed tree sloth. Of the midget horse and sipapu . . . the birthplace. Home of the evil gods.

"Look," she said, flushed with excitement, "you can see the trail. That's where I was, only a week ago."

Her face was pressed against the window, like a child's. He gazed not at the canyon but at the girl, at the coal-black lashes of her jeweled eyes, the slight arch of her nose, the cameo profile of lips and chin and throat, the curve of her breast under cashmere, her arm, her slender wrists and small brown hands. What is this delicate creature here beside me? Who is she? How could she ever have gone, alone, down through that dungeon labyrinth of rock and cactus and rattlesnakes, through the heat and silence, without me? That he had not been with her then seemed to him now like an absolute, forever-inconsolable loss.

The cliffs came up. The other rim passed below and they were again flying over the forest. Green meadows passed beneath them, a winding road, a few cars.

The plane dropped toward a landing strip on the edge of a natural clearing where a few cattle could be seen grazing. Gatlin felt the wheels bump on the hard earth, saw the trees flashing by on his right at ninety miles an hour. He waited for the tug of the brakes but felt instead an abrupt acceleration, heard the motor roar. Looking ahead over the pilot's shoulder, he saw a cow and calf ambling across the middle of the runway.

Well, he thought. Fine. So this is how it all ends. He felt the girl's hand squeezing his arm. He covered her hand with his own and felt a fatal, simple acquiescence, without fear. There would not even be time to tell her, to kiss her.

But they were in the air again and circling, the pilot looking back over his shoulder at the cattle. At the end of the strip was a parked bus and they could all clearly see the driver of the bus lounging against a fender, waiting, picking his teeth, watching the airplane.

Muttering, the pilot turned the plane and came back and dove toward the cattle at full throttle, buzzing over their heads at twenty feet. He waggled the plane's wings at the bus driver, who waved one hand in languid response, but made no move to clear the landing strip. The pilot's lips were moving and Gatlin knew what he must be saying, "The stupid sonofabitch." Twice more they circled and dove before the cattle drifted clear and the runway was safe for a landing.

Gatlin and Sandy were the last to climb out of the cabin of the plane. The pilot was talking to the bus driver, quietly.

"Feel all right?" Gatlin said to Sandy, helping her down from the wing step.

"Oh fine. Why not? He's a good pilot."

"Couldn't have done any better yourself, eh?"

She smiled. "That's right."

The pilot came back to the plane shaking his head, but grinned when Gatlin and the girl shook hands with him and thanked him for the dive bombing. They got into the bus, where the driver, sullen and silent, gave them no greeting but sped off at once for the road. Above the windshield was a metal plaque identifying their driver as one "Melvin E. Mundt: Safe, Reliable, Courteous."

"But stupid," Gatlin said to the girl. Smiling, she put one finger over her lips.

Gatlin stopped the driver near the parking lot at the head of the canyon trail. In Sandy's car they drove to the cafeteria for coffee before beginning the long trip—three hundred miles—around the canyon to their starting point on the other rim.

She had missed breakfast. He watched her eat, admiring the grace of her hands and the mildness of her manner, the softness of her voice when she spoke to him (a comely thing in woman). To Gatlin she was beginning to seem not only comely but also witty, intelligent, liberal—a princess. And a princess of that rarest and finest kind: an American princess.

Ah no, he told himself, no, no, never again. Stick to the old scheme, the wise and prudent master plan. But he was beginning to realize that he had a long way to go. Life is very long. The master plan in this light, on this sunny morning, appeared intolerably bleak. Not only bleak but stupid, cowardly. Like the grave.

They talked of the flight. They talked of the view of the canyon from the air, they spoke of deserts, mountains, seashores and cities. She thought Washington was a beautiful city. But she had never seen Stockholm on a winter evening. Or Naples from the Posilipo at any time. Or even San Francisco. All those scenes that Gatlin once had known and still loved (in moderation, to be sure) he now remembered with a new love, seeing them through the eyes of this suntanned, slim-boned, clear-eyed girl, so delicate and at the same time so hardy, so feminine, so comradely, so young, so terrifyingly young. He wanted to see it all again, with her, that world which he had thought he no longer needed or wanted. He even thought, in the heat of this strange enthusiasm, that he could enjoy coming back at evening through the catatonic crowds of Manhattan, under the river through the Tubes, to a cold-water flat in Hoboken, if she were there, waiting for him.

She said, "Why the Southwest?"

He told her. Admiring the shine in her half-wild eyes. The eyes of a doe. Told her the dreary tale, his melancholy memoirs, the crooked chronicle of his days. Admiring the span and arch of her brown eyebrows, the subtle blue shading of her eyelids, her fresh translucent skin, the pulse at the base of her throat. Told her not the whole story, of course, but an outline of it, a diagram. The words as always so poor an imitation of the reality; not even in fact an imitation at all but a different reality, making what little he remembered of his life something apart and separate, in a different world. He even liked the old sweater she was wearing and the big wooden bangles on her wrist. I must get her a bracelet, he decided, a band of Navajo silver.

"Why the Southwest?"

"Because it's clean."

"How domestic."

"I like the simplicity of the landscape. It soothes my nerves. I like the local beer. Coors. A-1."

"How plebeian."

"I like the men and women who have lived out here long enough to acquire some of the character of the country . . . men of pride and independence with the look of great distances in their eyes."

"Real estate speculators?"

"Yes. And stalwart foresters with spirits too brave and generous ever to yield. To melancholy."

"Are they really like that?"

"No. You know they're not."

"I know. They drink too much, most of them."

"Or talk too much."

"Or too little," she said.

"Aye, lass."

He was silent.

"Poor old Will Gatlin." She was laughing at him. "Will he or won't he?"

"Never leap at foregone conclusions."

"I refuse to accept foregone conclusions. What are we talking about?"

"That's the spirit, now you're talking. Anything is possible."

"Anything?"

"Anything. Even happiness."

"And sorrow?"

"That of course is always likely. They say it's beautiful, sorrow. At least in others."

"The tragic view of life?"

"Yes, now you've got it. Heroic resignation to the suffering of others."

They both fell silent for a while, smiling mysteriously at each other (weren't they?) over the white coffee cups and the white cloth on the table. Across the distance.

"How long have you been living alone?" she asked.

"All my life."

"Haven't you ever been in love?"

"Ah well, that too, all my life. Isn't it the same with you?"

"Yes."

They left the cafeteria and drove slowly through the forest, through great open meadows where the deer came out to graze, past lady tourists picking roadside flowers, past old stockmen's cabins rotting into ruin, past a fire tower and ranger station (where they halted briefly to paint mustachios on Smokey the Bear) and then down through a thinning growth of pine and pinyon and juniper toward the open country. He stopped the car at a lookout point on the brink of the plateau, far off the highway.

Below the escarpment, fierce and glowing under the noon sun, stretching eastward for as far as they could see toward dim blue mesas and volcanic peaks, lay the desert. They were glad to get out of the car and stand there on the edge of things for some time, arms around each other, not speaking.

"Say something," she said at last. "Something wise."

"The yawning abyss. It makes us sleepy."

"Okay. But it reminds me of a poem: 'Yonder all before us lie, Deserts of vast eternity.'"

"Very good. Marvelous."

She looked at him suspiciously. "You know it, don't you?"

"Yes." He pulled her close and kissed her on the forehead. "All of it. I know it by heart. I like your bangs, Sandy. I like your sunburned nose. You have a good strong nose, you know that? A nose with force, spirit, a patrician nose."

"Thank you. It's a functional nose too, it works. And you, you look like an old beat-up sheepherder."

"I'm really a prospector. Without any prospects. Searching for that mother lode."

"Maybe you just need a mother."

"Right now, lass, I need some lunch."

She opened her pack and brought out the wine and cheese and bread. While he uncorked the bottle, with more success this time, she sawed off two slices from the dark solid loaf.

"That looks like true bread," he said. "Where'd you get it?"

"I made it." She looked at him proudly. "I baked it myself."

"You are marvelous. You are not only a pretty girl in the process of becoming a beautiful woman, you are a person of wit and talent. You are a personage."

"You are drunk already, Mr. Gatlin."

The red desert shimmered in the heat, three thousand feet below. But where they sat, on the warm rock in mountain sunlight, the air remained cool and comfortable, sparkling and clear and exciting. A hummingbird darted past them in a flash of iridescence, swung back, and hovered before a blossoming scarlet pentstemon, wings beating invisibly, and probed the heart of the flower. Locusts whirred nearby in the cliff rose and buckbrush. In the middle distance a black buzzard with white-trimmed wings soared in lazy circles above something dead or dying or waiting to die on the plain below.

"Brother Gatlin," she pointed out, indicating the vulture, "in his reincarnated state."

"Do you believe in reincarnation?"

"I believe in everything. What do you believe in?"
"Nothing," he confessed.
"How banal. Nothing at all?"
"Nothing but wine and bread and cheese."
"That's what I thought. Have some more cheese."
"Have some more wine."

They ate and drank, sitting close together on the white limestone wall above the drop-off, and watched the blue shadows of the clouds fold slowly over the folds of the cliff and advance eastward into the desert. Far away, on the horizon, loomed a dome-shaped mountain.

"Another holy place," he was saying. "Another navel of the earth, sacred to the Navajo."
"Teach me some Navajo."
"*Ya-ha-la-ni.*"
"What does that mean?"
"It's a very affectionate greeting."
"What does it mean?"
"I love you."
"Okay. What else do you know?"
"*Ch'indy begay.*"
"And what does that mean?"
"Son of the devil."
"That's nice too. *Ya-ha-la-ni, ch'indy begay.* I love you, son of the devil. Very nice. You have a very useful vocabulary, Mr. Gatlin."
"Call me Will."
"Will."
"Sandy, god damn it."
"God damn it, Will."
"Thatta girl. Say it again. God *damn* it."
"God *damn* it."
"Christ."
"Christ."
"Jesus."

"Jesus."

"Very good." He hugged her tightly and nosed around in her soft, shining hair, bit her tenderly on the ear, kissed her eyebrow, her cheek, her mouth, tasted the sweetness of her tongue.

"What do you call that?" she asked.

"What do you mean?"

"Well . . . that business with the tongue."

"Speaking in tongues."

"Wise guy. Seriously. Please tell me, I want to know."

"What's the matter with this Lawrence Turner the Third? What do girls learn at Goucher anyway?"

"Will you tell me, please."

He smiled at her. "I call it . . . the cunning lingo of love."

"I'll remember that. Cunning lingo. Okay. Now what?"

"This."

Ah, she's beautiful, he thought. She's homely as a dove. She's lovely as a lark. She's sweet as a song, my bird, my bird.

They descended into the desert by stages, like birds, swinging wide on the curves, floating down through plane on plane of heat and color and form, under the wide wild candescent sky.

They paused near the top of the last grade in the highway to assist a visitor from another land, from a place named Alabama, Heart of Dixie, whose car stood vaporlocked on the shoulder of the road. They gave him water to drink and a water-soaked rag for his overheated fuel pump. The charity of lovers. They stopped again down on the desert plain to give a ride to a hitchhiking Indian. The powerful odor of muscatel, hogan and juniper smoke filled the car until they dropped him off, as requested, at the next trading post. On through the red wasteland, into a burned-out region of snakeweed and prickly pear, off on a dusty side road and down to the shore of the river.

He parked the car in the shade of a giant willow tree. Passed her the nearly empty wine bottle. The river, a blend of plankton green and ocher, moved quietly before them. Toward what sounded like a remote, sustained catastrophe.

"Finish it," he said.
"You want to get me drunk?"
"Yes."
"You want to seduce me."
"Yes."
"But I'm—"
"I know."
"I'm a virgin."
"I know. I forgive you."
"You're terrible."
"Yes."
"Will you please go away somewhere while I put on my bathing suit?"
"I'll be waiting for you in the water."

He walked over the boulders and sand to a hard sandy beach, undressed and plunged out of the stunning heat into the river. The water was cold and dense, with a strong current. He swam against the current for a while, stretching his muscles against the power of the river, then let it carry him aside and into the backwash. He stood waist deep in the water and watched her come, dancing quickly over the hot sand. She wore a two-piece sort of thing, little more than a bikini; her body was slender, brown, graceful; her gleaming hair, tangled by the wind, came down and covered the freckles on her shoulders, the tiny mole on her back.

"The sand is so hot!"
"Run."

She raced to the edge of the water, dove in and swam

toward him. He caught and embraced her, kissed her, dragged her into the deep.

"You're crazy," she said. "What's this?"

"That's me."

"You're naked."

"Yes, stark raving naked."

"You're awful. Let me go."

"Never."

But she was a better swimmer than he was. She slipped from his arms, disappeared, came up ten yards away, laughing at him, and struck out toward the middle of the river.

"No!" he shouted. "Don't go out there!"

She stopped, paddled in circles, looking at him. Slowly the river carried her away.

"The rapids!" he shouted.

She came back, carving a path across the current with smooth, regular strokes. Wet and shining as a seal, she stood before him, her breast heaving, wiping the water from her eyes.

"What rapids?"

"Around the first bend. Don't you hear it?"

She listened. "Yes. Oh that's what that noise is."

Constant in the air hung a low vibration, the sound of spray and thunder and madness, like the sea, like the roaring of a distant multitude.

"The current is very strong out there. It could carry you right down into the rapids."

"I'm a good swimmer."

"Not that good."

"What's beyond the rapids?"

"More rapids. Three hundred miles of wild river and a hundred rapids, each more terrible than the one before. All down there in the canyon, in that dark inner gorge. Where the river goes underground, into Hades."

"How romantic."

"Exactly. And I'm your demon lover."

"Do you believe in plutonic love?"

He laughed joyously. "Plutonic? Yes!"

"Have I got it wrong?" She smiled in uncertainty. "Isn't that the right word?"

The green-gold water of the river surged past their wet and shining bodies. A dazzling light streamed down and exploded in a million glints of fire on the roil and play of the waves. On the shore tamarisk and willow bent with the breeze, beyond the edge of the glittering sand. Heat waves floated in glassy layers before the face of the cliffs, veiling the distance and the hot rosy radiance of stone. From downriver came the low roar, like an endless, tireless, fanatic applause, of the rapids. Under the listening sky.

They were alone.

16

IN THE LATE AFTERNOON, early evening, the sun yielding at last, they lay on the sand under the willow tree and watched their supper cook on the clear slow passion of burning juniper. One lizard crawled with care down the veined face of a granite boulder, watching them, and slipped with a twitch of tapering tail into the black shadow beneath the rock. They scooped up the fine river sand in their hands and let it flow through their fingers. Talking quietly.

The river seemed to have slackened somewhat in its flow, the sound of the falls was farther away. Sunlight reflected from the clouds broke on the hard metallic surface of the water downstream. Doves called. A blue heron launched itself into the air from its perch on the cliff and swung heavily up the canyon.

"I'm afraid."

"Yes."

"Later? Is it all right?"

"Yes."

Miles overhead, a world away, three gray shapes passed silently, like sharks, and trailed their ragged plumes of vapor across the darkening, tranquil sky.

17   Dear Willy,

Another day, another dolor.

It has been said, not without justice, that the tangled affairs of men proceed not from pleasure to pleasure but from hope to desperate hope. And that the concept of the infinite can most easily be grasped by contemplating human stupidity. So it is, lad, and thus it goes with your erst friend and comrade A. Ballantine, gent.

They flee from me that once did seek me out. My delicious Darnelle, she of the undulant, abundant not to say redundant mammaries, has flown my coop and left me stranded high and dry, master of my own dunghill and nothing much else.

Of course she's replaceable—there's fifty thousand waiting for me in this one city alone; if there's anything the good Lord provides it's a multiplicity, not to say a superfluity, of cunt. But for how long can one go on plucking the fruits of this tree? Will they still love me when I am old and bald and fat and impotent? Will I care? There are times when I lie awake at night pondering this question. The greater your dreams the more terrible your nightmares. Beware your wishes for they might come true. Etc., etc.

I console myself with these words from Santayana: "No truly masculine man ever failed to nourish in his bosom the desire to possess many women." Santayana, mind you; *Santayana* said that.

Perhaps I should switch to a different age bracket, let the chicks alone, try the post-menopausal. E.g., I've got the nicest, sweetest, cleanest naïve little old landlady here: she has blue hair, green varicose veins and a mouthful of old gold choppers. And a bod too: 45-55-65, if she's an inch. As wise old Ben Franklin used to say, "The best part of a woman is the last part to decay." I'm losing my mind thinking about it.

Us crazy spiders spin asymmetric webs.

Well, how's the Olde Masturbator from the Faraway Hills? Is it really too much to demand even a single letter from you? My Gawd man you can take those boxing gloves off long enough to write me a letter can't you? Discipline, Willy, discipline—that's the secret. Like me.

Well, life goes on. *Pourquoi?* You may well ask.

Yrs. forever, *usque ad finem,* in the glorious fraternity of the damned.

—Red Dog

18

ONE SMALL PUFF of smoke against the dark green of the ridge. Which fades and passes out of vision even as he watches. But he has marked the place with his eye and takes a reading. Waits, the glasses in hand. With infinite and infinitely casual lassitude a second puff of blue-gray woodsmoke forms at the same point, rises and hovers in the air like a silent exclamation mark above the landscape. He verifies the first reading, checks the vertical angle, takes a look through the glasses and locates the site precisely on the survey map.

Picks up the microphone on the radiotelephone set.

"Seven eighty, seven eighty-one, fire call."

"Seven eighty. Go ahead."

"Have a little smoke for you, Wendell, at fourteen degrees and five minutes. Looks like a snag. About ten miles from here."

The fire dispatcher repeats the description of the fire and its location. "How's the rest, Will?"

"Okay, so far," says Gatlin.

Grand banks of cumulus-nimbus clouds fill the southern hemisphere of the sky. From some of them hang trailing virgas, curtains of rain which evaporate midway between heaven and earth. In the evening there are more lightning strikes, scattered, sporadic, whose distance from the tower he measures by the sweeping second hand of the clock, waiting for the sound of thunder. He takes a reading on each strike and records the location. The sun goes down behind a mountainous range of clouds spreading northward across the west.

He pauses outside on the catwalk before descending. In the twilight of the forest below the quiet deer forage across the clearing, all facing in the same direction, like cattle at pasture, like carp in dark water. Between the distant mutter of rolls of thunder he hears a keening noise, the thin continual dirgelike chorus of the spotted tree toads excited by the sense of coming rain.

Across the clearing, beyond the cistern and table, beyond the sawn stump, the ax, the woodpile, the horseshoe court, is the head of the path. Fixing his gaze on that turn where the trail emerges from the mixed light and darkness of the aspens, he can hear her voice, can see again the pale slender figure of the girl coming for the first time alone to his cabin. Across the chasm of time and an inconsolable loss he sees the soft glow of her hair, her timid smile.

"Sandy?"

The deer lift their heads at the sound of his voice, stare up at him not in surprise, not in fear, but with a calm, unruffled, almost complacent consideration, as at a noise familiar, harmless, but infrequent. As if a tree had spoken, rubbing one dead limb against another.

The sound is not repeated. One by one, after an interval of motionless and untroubled waiting, the deer lower their heads and continue feeding in the silent gathering pool of darkness in the clearing at the foot of the tower.

19 The trysting log.

Near the junction of his path with the road, the public road, they had their private mailbox. A hollow log, half decayed, flat on the ground. Surrounded by the pines.

Sometimes, when he looked into the opening, he would find a many-folded slip of paper. With words. Words.

> My darling Will,
> I think of you, sweetheart, night and day. I miss you so very much. When will I see you again?

> *Mon ange, mon cheri, mon berger . . .
> je t'adore! je t'aime!*
>
> —S.

To which he might, in a word, reply.

> S.:
> *Venez.*
> —W.

20

FOR A TIME, until the girl, there had been another whom he sometimes visited on his days off, driving the ninety miles south to the city to spend a weekend in her apartment.

"Help me with the kids," she yelled.

He sighed heavily, set his new pipe in the ashtray and went with iron feet into the bathroom, where Rosalie was bathing the three children of a long-gone father. The two smallest were in the tub, splashing water over each other, over the walls, over their mother, while the oldest boy scrambled naked, wet and giggling around the room. Will caught him and thrust him, laughing and struggling, into the tub.

"You do that again I'll stick your head under the water!" Rosalie screamed at the child.

Will winked at the boy, shook his head at Rosalie. He put his arm around her shoulders and took her aside for a minute. "Rosie," he said, "don't make threats like that." Very softly he said, "You don't want the boy to be afraid of the water, do you? He'll never learn to swim."

"He drives me crazy," she grumbled. "I could kill him when he does things like that."

"Easy, easy . . ."

"Sure, it's easy for you to say that. You don't have to spend every day and every night with them."

"I know." He stroked her shoulders, her hair. "You're right. Let me help you."

Together they bathed and toweled the children: two dark little boys, a girl too small for her age with fair brown hair and lustrous little brown shoebutton eyes. Arturo, Eliseo, Consuela, all three beautiful and quick as squirrels. He helped their mother wrestle them into pajamas and by himself, in one dancing armload, carried all three into their bedroom and put them to bed, turned out the lights and told them stories, long and surreal and improvised stories, until they were quiet and their eyes closed. He gave each a kiss and a firm hug and left them sleeping.

The woman waited for him in the front room, which she called her living room. Through the curtains of the window he could see the neon lights of the street below and the passing lights of automobiles. Rosalie sat with her knees drawn up on the couch, watching the television screen, where a glamorous young woman with immaculate complexion, golden hair and a face of impossible Nordic symmetry was peddling shampoo. The face in the blue box smiled at them relentlessly, mercilessly, with wide red lips and gleaming teeth, and kept on talking and talking about shampoo, combing and recombing her golden hair, a sick, enslaved Rapunzel.

"I wish I looked like that," Rosalie said.

"That lady is a whore," he said. "You wouldn't want to look like a whore. And live in a box."

"How do you know she's a whore?"

"Look what she's doing. She looks like a whore. And the worst kind too—all show and no delivery."

"You think she sleeps with the producer?"

"Not any more. She doesn't have to now. Besides, who would want her? She looks carnivorous—all those sharp teeth. She's a castrator."

"You honestly think so?"

"Yes," he lied. "How about a beer?"

Rosalie got up and went to the kitchen. While she was gone Gatlin turned down the volume of the set so low that it became inaudible. He enjoyed television but only when silent. Television should be seen and not heard. The commercial over, the show began. Rosalie came back with two open cans of beer and sat close beside him. They stared at the silent shadows in the tube. Outside, in the street, auto horns burst into a flurry of protest, subsided.

"And what am I?" Rosalie asked.

"What are you?"

"Am I a whore too?"

One arm around her, he lowered his beer. "No, you are not a whore."

"Will you marry me?"

"No."

"Then I must be a whore."

"No you are not."

"What am I?"

He squeezed her close. "You're Rosie. You're a good woman. You're a good mother, most of the time except when you lose your temper, and even that's understandable."

"That ain't enough."

"You're the only woman I know I give a damn about."

"Is that what you call love?"

"Yes."

"Marry me."

"No."

She pushed herself up from the couch, went to the television, turned up the volume. Her broad solid figure blocked his view of the screen. She came back and sat down again beside him, letting her body fall heavily onto the cushions.

"Might as well hear the show," she said.

"We could make love."

"Will you ever marry me?"

He drank some more beer. "No. I'll never marry anybody. Again. I'm not qualified to make any woman a decent husband."

"I think you'd make a wonderful husband."

"It's nice to think so." He put the beer can on the floor and embraced her, kissed her. She had a round plump face, still pretty, barely beginning to reveal the erosion of time and too much hard work, too much anxiety. Dark rings beneath her lovely violet eyes gave her a melancholy beauty; her flesh was rich and soft, smelling of lilac, but overripe, faintly corrupt, as if the cruel process of decay had already begun.

"Well," she said, "if you won't marry me I guess you might as well make love to me."

"What do you think I'm doing?"

"I was thinking about something else. You wanta turn out the lights?"

"Yes."

They coupled there on the couch in the metallic glow of the television. Rapunzel returned, watching and grinning at them, swinging her magnificent hair from side to side, crooning and swooning, peddling her wares, while Rosalie with all the clamor and predictability of an alarm clock came once, and came again, as Gatlin performed his duty.

She fell asleep. He carried her to her bed, covered her

with a blanket and left her there, slack-jawed and open-mouthed, exhausted and fulfilled, snoring deep into whatever her dreams must be. He went back to the couch in the front room, finished the beer, pulled on his clothes. The television set was still muttering over its problems; he turned the volume all the way down before going out.

Into the friendly neighborhood bar, where he had to stand aside at the doorway for a moment as two giant cops in helmets and guns and black leather dragged out an unconscious, bloodied Indian. Gatlin entered, moved through smoke, confusion, bodies and the howling of a mighty jukebox up to the bar.

Beside him stood an old man with high cheekbones, skin like saddle leather and a Mongolian mustache. He wore a tall black hat with a silver band and looked like Kubla Khan; he smelled like that corner of the corral where the water trough sets. He was splendid, and drunk, and able to stand.

"*Ya-ta-hay, hosteen,*" said Gatlin. "How's the sheep business?"

The old man smiled and replied in the only English he knew. "Fucking good."

"What're you drinking, Peshlakai?"

"Fucking good."

"Okay, I'll go along with that." Gatlin ordered two bourbons. "What's new in Dot Klish Canyon?"

"Fucking good."

"If there's anything better they're not selling it on television, that's for sure." The drinks appeared. *"Salud."* They touched glasses, drank. "Tell me about life," Gatlin said.

The old man wiped his mustache and grinned. "Fucking good."

A new fight began near the jukebox when a man named Jesus, Jesus Apodaca, a sheepherder, pulled a knife on a truckdriver named Soderlund. He should not have done that. The barmaid dialed the police again; the bartender, sighing, reached under the bar for his thirty-eight-ounce solid ash Louisville Slugger autographed personally by Harmon Killebrew.

21

AFTER SUNDOWN they left the river and drove homeward, tired and drowsy, through the cooling desert night. The highway was empty, all theirs. Unidentifiable birds fluttered across their advance, narrowly missing the car. A pair of eyes like opals burned ahead, on the shoulder, reflecting the car lights; a bobcat loped from right to left over the pavement, disappeared. They stopped for coffee at the cafe near the highway junction, trying to keep themselves awake. Still nearly eighty miles to go.

"I should phone Larry," the girl said.

"More coffee?"

"No thanks." She looked at the clock on the wall. "He usually calls me about this time."

Gatlin said nothing.

"He might worry."

Gatlin said nothing.

"Although he hasn't written to me for two weeks. So why should I call him? Do I owe him a call?"

Gatlin rubbed his eyes. He was tired, and reasonably happy, and sleepy, and a little indifferent. A long day. Let the wench fight this one out on her own. All he really wanted at present was to get into bed. *With* her, of course, if possible, but anyway into bed.

"Do you suppose they have a phone here? I could call collect."

"They have rooms here," he said. "Reasonable rates."

The sunburn deepened on her rosy face. She smiled and lowered her eyes. "Is that what you're thinking about?"

"It's very simple. I want to make love to you, Sandy. Then go to sleep. And wake up in the morning with you in my arms and make love to you again."

Slowly she shook her head. "Oh Will . . ."

"Shall I take a room?"

"No. Please. I can't. Not yet."

"All right."

"You'd better take us home."

"Okay." He got up, paid for the coffee. As they went out the door he said, "What about your phone call?"

She sighed, taking his arm and leaning on him. "I'm so tired. Tomorrow."

They drove on, under the diamond-bright web of stars. The highway climbed out of the desert, up onto the plateau and into the cold night of the forest. The girl stretched out on the front seat beside him, resting her sleepy head on his lap. He placed his free hand on the downy-sweatered mound of her breast. She clasped both her hands over his, keeping it there.

"I'm *so* sleepy," she said.

"Go to sleep," he said. The strength of his desire would at least help keep him awake.

When he finally reached the village, near midnight, and stopped the car under the yellow pines beside her place, the girl was sound asleep. He woke her as gently as he could.

"Sandy, you're home."

Slowly she opened her eyes. He helped her out of the car and up the steps of the porch to her front door. She opened the door, then turned to face him, hesitating. "Will."

He kissed her. "Good night." And started to go.

"Will? You must be awfully tired."

He smiled. "I am."

"I wish . . . When will I see you again?"

"Whenever you want to."

"You'll come?"

"No."

"No? What does that mean?"

"I want you to come to me. You know where I live."

"When?"

"In the evening."

"In the evening?"

"Bring your toothbrush."

She stared at him, her wide eyes glistening in the darkness, her mouth open. He put his hands on her breasts, kissed her again and walked away.

22

Colorado Springs, Colo.

DEAR MR. GATLIN:

My fiancée Miss MacKenzie informs me that she has allowed herself to become involved emotionally with you. The exact extent of this involvement she does not make clear.

Is it necessary for me to point out to you, sir, that Sandy is hardly more than a child? She tells me that you are what she calls "an older man." If this is true, it seems apparent that you are taking advantage of her immaturity and lack of experience for ends of your own, which, under the circumstances, seem to be of questionable honor.

I want you to understand that I intend to marry Miss MacKenzie in the fall when I complete my flight training. I trust that you will understand my feelings in this matter and will immediately break off whatever sort of relation you have made with her. Assuming that you are, sir, a gentleman, it should not be necessary for me to communicate with you any further in this regard. If on the other hand you are not a gentleman, which I regret to say seems more likely in this case, then I shall hold you fully responsible for whatever happens and shall take steps of whatever severity may be required to correct this unfortunate situation.

                              Yours sincerely,
                              [Signed]
                              Lawrence J. Turner III
                              Cadet Pilot, USAF

23

DRIVING BEYOND the little beach, which he remembers well, too well, and past the big willow tree where even now he can find, if he wants to search, the blackened stones of a fireplace, he continues for another mile to the end of the road. Where things have changed. There is a ranger station here now, and a commercial marina with store, docks, a launching ramp and boats for rent.

Gatlin chooses a small boat of the type called whaler, double-hulled fiberglass, with a powerful eighty-horsepower outboard motor. Alone, he races up the river at full throttle, through the afternoon, over a waterway that gleams under the sun like polished brass, golden and dazzling, under the red cliffs of the canyon. The wake of his boat flashes in the light, spreading from wall to wall, splashing against the rocky shore and against the white sand of lonely beaches overgrown with young willows and tamarisk. Against the wind blowing in his face, above the roar of the motor, he sings.

> "Rejoice, Columbia's sons, rejoice,
> To tyrants never bend the knee,
> But join with heart and mind and voice
> For Jefferson! And Liberty!"

In the middle of the channel he twists the boat to the left and works his way around a sandbar into a cove he knows and likes; shutting off the motor, he ties the bow line to a tree growing out over the bank, baits a hook with salmon eggs. The fish are biting; he catches several catfish and a couple of rainbow trout but all too small. Planted fish, hatchery fish. He throws them back into the water.

The heat becomes oppressive. He strips and dives over the side, swims around the boat twice and then to the beach, where he walks up and down for a while, naked as Adam. Birds flit darkly through the willow thickets, chattering. A hawk sails overhead in the strip of blue between the cliffs. He lies in the shade, on the warm sand, unable to sleep, dreaming awake.

Late in the afternoon he swims back to the boat, climbs aboard, casts loose and lets it drift with the current down the river. Half in shade, half in sun, he sprawls on the seat and watches through half-closed eyes the slow ponderous movement of the canyon rim a thousand feet above turning against the sky. Carved in that monumental rock he sees alcoves and arches, pillars and buttresses, and on the skyline the profiles of blind, silent, implacable gods, bird gods in stone with the masks of hawks.

A beaver swims by, headed upstream, passing within six feet of the boat. Gatlin watches it go. On shore he sees another, standing, balanced like a tripod on its hind legs and tail, preening its sleek head with the two dexterous forepaws.

The sound of human voices. He is floating past the marina, out of the upper canyon and through an opening in the cliffs toward the lower canyon. Toward the great canyon. Already he can hear, from a mile ahead, the first dull murmur of the rapids. A shout from onshore.

Gatlin starts the motor and turns upriver toward the docks. Hesitates, changes his mind and turns the boat around again. He switches the fuel line from the near-empty tank to a full one, puts on a lifejacket and stands up behind the wheel in order to see more easily what lies directly ahead. Slowing the motor to idling speed, he bears for the smooth shining tongue of the first rapids.

A wave curls before him. He passes around the first rock, a pale slab of limestone dim beneath the green water, and into the rapids. The boat yaws and pitches, shipping water by the bucketful. Between two rocks and into a trough in the waves. He guns the motor as a rolling wave crashes into the boat, setting everything loose afloat. His shoes and socks, his rod and tackle box and water jug float around his ankles. Beyond the rapids, in quiet water again, he unscrews the drain plug in the stern and lets the motor pump the boat dry.

Cruising on down the river, between gravel bars and submerged boulders, crashing through more minor rapids like the first, he enters deeper and deeper into the gorge, into deep shadows under a sky charged with evening sunlight, toward the beginning of the wilderness.

Around a bend. Not far ahead he can now see what looks like the end of the river. The water seems to come to a sudden fall or dropping-off place beyond which the river cannot be seen. Along this edge hovers a mist of spray, pale against the darkness beyond, and into the mist, at irregular intervals, curling waves leap from below.

Down there. Gatlin stares into the chaos before him. Down there, he thinks. Where? How far? Somewhere, down in there, a hundred miles below.

He beaches the boat and walks along the shore toward the rapids, clambering over a delta of boulders big as houses washed down from a side canyon. On one of these, surrounded by swirling water, he sits and contemplates the heart of the tumbling river. Fangs of rock split the current as it drops from ledge to ledge, descending twenty feet in a distance shorter than a football field. There are waves in there twelve feet high, holes and explosions in the water, a whirlpool of foam and fury. He might if extremely lucky get the boat down through here; he could never get it back again.

Gatlin is tempted. Why not, he thinks. Go on. Into it. Keep going. All the way into the underworld. Somewhere down in there she may still be alive, waiting for you, hoping for you, dreaming of you as you dream of her. Living on what? On watercress and mesquite beans and the bloom of the sacred datura. On hope and memory.

No. There is no remedy. The river sings, a mad chaotic babble of many voices . . .

Through the twilight he walks slowly back to the boat, deafened by the dull deep roar of the rapids. He almost blunders into a rattlesnake. Stopping suddenly, he is seized for a moment by the primeval fear.

The snake is a diamondback, six feet long and thick as his forearm; agitated, hostile, it lies coiled in the middle of the path, the heavy spade-shaped head aloft and weaving from side to side, ready to strike. The tail vibrates in nervous frenzy, inaudible, however, against the uproar of the river.

Gatlin backs off a step. He crouches low and peers directly into the eyes of the snake. He places his hand on a loose stone.

"Cousin," he cries, "what have you done with her?"

The bleak and dusty eyes stare back at him, the thin black tongue slips in and out as the snake attempts to sense the nature of this unknown danger.

"What have you done with her?" Gatlin cries again. He lifts the stone, advances a step.

On guard, ready to lunge, the big rattlesnake retreats slowly toward the side of the path, toward the shelter of the cactus and tumbled rocks.

Gatlin drops the stone, lifts empty hands palm upward toward the snake.

"Where is she?" he begs. "Where is she?"

24

DURING MOST of the afternoon it rained, with lightning bombarding the forest on all sides of the tower. He recorded thirty strikes in his range before the storm moved on, leaving behind a sky spread with enormous shoals of ragged, fiery clouds that flared for an hour after the sun had gone down, smoldering like banked coals against the yellow sky. As darkness settled over the forest the clouds gathered again and a fine drizzling rain, without lightning, began to fall.

He was about to descend from the tower when he saw the pale figure, faint and wraithlike as smoke, coming up the trail through the dark of the woods.

"Sandy?"

The girl waved. Gatlin ran down the stairways and met her near the door of the cabin. Her white macintosh was covered with raindrops. She took off her hat and shook free a stream of water. He stared at the soft glow of her hair, the brightness of her eyes.

"Well?" she said. She smiled timidly. "Here I am. I even brought my toothbrush."

He gaped at her. "You really came. You're really here."

"Pinch me if you don't believe it."

"Yes." He put his hands on her arms, squeezed. "Wonderful. You really came."

"Yes I did."

They stood there in the fine rain, like idiots, staring at each other. Finally he shook himself alive. "Come on in. Let's go in, it's raining again." He led her into the dark cabin, where the smell of woodsmoke and fried bacon mingled with the odors of the rain and the wind and the rain-soaked forest outside. He struck a match and lit the lantern hanging from the rafters, carefully turning up the wick before replacing the globe. The sound of the rain falling steadily on the sheet metal roof vibrated through the interior.

"I ate supper two hours ago," he said. "Are you hungry?"

"No."

"Take off that wet coat. Here, give it to me." He hung it on a nail. Under the coat she wore only a light dress; her arms were bare and covered with goose pimples. "You're cold," he said. She nodded and shivered. He took a heavy sweater from another nail in the wall and draped it over her shoulders. "Here, I'll stoke up this fire." He poked the fire in the stove, added chunks of wood. "Coffee?" he said. "Tea?"

"If it's already made."

"You bet it is." He pulled off a stovelid and set the kettle directly over the flames. Hesitating. "Look," he said, pulling a bottle from the cupboard, "have a slug of the old firewater. This'll warm you up quick." He poured a shot in a tin cup, adding a little water.

"I don't know . . ."

"Try it."

She sipped gingerly, made a grimace. "Awful."

"Not bad, eh. Take some more."

She sipped a little more. "Awful."

"It sure is. Drink it all." He pulled a chair close to the stove, opened the oven door. "Sit here, Sandy. Stick your feet in the oven. Go on, it's not hot yet. How's that? Feel better?"

She nodded.

"You're nervous," he said.

She nodded. "Yes. I'm scared."

"So am I."

"I never spent a night with a man before."

"I know. And I never spent a night with you before. That makes us even." He smiled at her and squeezed her shoulder. "The way to do it," he said, "the only easy way, we'll have to get just a little bit drunk. First. Okay?"

"Okay."

"So drink up." He tipped the bottle to his lips, drank. "My God. Firewater. Wait a minute." He went to the cupboard again, came back with a much smaller bottle with a starry label. "This is better." He took the cup from her, threw the contents onto the floor beneath the cupboard. "For the mouse." He poured a little brandy liqueur into her cup. "Try that, you'll like it. Forgot I had this stuff. Isn't that better?"

"Yes."

"Ready for your tea?" She was. He poured a mug for her and gave it to her. "Sugar? Yes? Cream? No? That's good because frankly we haven't got any cream on hand at this time. Warm enough?"

"Yes."

He poured some brandy for himself, pulled up the second chair and sat beside her, putting his booted feet also into the oven. The rain fell steadily, loudly on the roof. The fire murmured in the stove.

She began to look around. "What are the guns for?"

"Shooting."

"Are they loaded?"

"Maybe."

"What do you shoot?"

"Things."

"Things? What things?"

"Well, deer in season. My season."

"Oh no. How could you shoot those beautiful animals? That's horrible. It's cruel."

"I don't think so. One shot and they're dead."

"How can you be sure?"

"I put out a block of salt about ten yards from that window." He grinned at her. "Never miss."

"You're awful. Is that what you call sport?"

"No, I'm not a sportsman."

"How can you do a thing like that?"

"Well, I like the meat. I don't make much money at this job and in the winter I usually don't make any money at all. I need the meat in order to eat. So when I leave here in the fall I generally take a few sides of venison with me."

"It sounds terribly illegal."

"It is. I'm not a good citizen."

"What do you do in the winters?"

He lit his pipe. He thought for a while. "Nothing."

"Except eat your meat."

"Right. Except eat my meat."

"Maybe you visit your lady friends." Now she was looking at his pictures. "Are those your children?"

He looked where she was pointing. "The older boy on

the left is. The others ain't. The lady with the blond hair was my wife. She lives in New York."

"She's beautiful. She looks like a model.

Gatlin said nothing.

"Who's the other woman?"

"A friend."

The girl was silent for a moment. "Just a friend? Are you in love with her?"

"Sometimes I wish I was." He put more wood in the stove. "Like more tea?"

"But you're not?"

"I'm not. More tea?"

"Yes please. And would you put a little of that—is it brandy?—in it, please."

They listened for a while to the perfect music of the wind and rain and night. To the fire and the simmering kettle.

"You told me you were a teacher," she said. "But you never told me why you quit."

"Didn't I?" He sighed. "Christ . . ."

She touched his arm. "Am I . . . Do you think I'm too nosey?"

He smiled at her and kissed her on the forehead. "Sandy, by God, I think thou art fairer than the evening air, Clad in the beauty of a thousand stars."

"Shelley? Keats? Wordsworth? No? Shakespeare? No?"

"Byron."

"Oh. Am I too nosey?"

"No you're not. And the reason I quit teaching is because my students kept getting in trouble. Everything I told them was wrong."

"I don't believe you."

"My ignorance was terrifying." He stared at the flames glowing behind the vents of the firebox. "An abyss."

"I don't believe you."

She leaned her head against his shoulder. He put an arm around her and drew her close. A gust of wind shook the trees and the washpan on the outside wall swung back and forth over the slabs.

"What was that?"

"Nothing. Just a pan on the wall. A little more of this?" He tipped the brandy bottle to her cup.

"Yes. Are there bears here?"

"A few." He kissed her, got up, went to the bed and zippered two heavy sleeping bags together. She watched him in silence.

"Should've told me you were coming tonight," he said. "I'd have had our bed all ready for you."

"I didn't plan to come. But I found your note."

"And came."

"And just came."

"With your toothbrush." He fluffed up a pair of pillows.

She smiled. "Well, I thought I *might* come. Can I help you?"

"All finished. Want to get in?"

"I don't know. Maybe I shouldn't." She stared at the bed, at him, at the dim yellow lantern light on the walls. She took another sip from her cup.

"Well," he said, "you're welcome to sleep on the floor." He smiled at her, paused. "I'm going out for a while."

He put on a hat and jacket and stepped out into the cold, rainy night. The air felt fresh and sweet; down in the marsh the amphibia were singing madly. He walked to the far edge of the clearing, through the drizzle, and listened for a while to the sounds of the rain, the forest, the night.

When he returned to the cabin she was in the bed. He added wood to the fire and reached for the lamp.

"Don't turn out the light," she said. He waited. "I want to watch you undress," she explained.

"All right." He began to take off his clothes.

"I want to look at you."

"All right."

Buried in the covers up to her chin, she watched him as he stripped off his underwear. "You have a fine body, I think."

He did not answer. Naked, he brushed his teeth, spat a mouthful of water and toothpaste out the door, came back, turned down the wick of the lamp. Slowly the light faded out. The fire in the stove cast a faint yellow glow through the room. He slid into the double bag with the girl and without a word clasped his arms around her, entwined his legs with hers. She trembled in his embrace, her vibrant body burning with an animal heat and freshness which astonished, delighted, amazed him; he had forgotten so much. Tasting the sweetness of her mouth, he found her cheeks wet with tears.

"Hey . . . you're crying. What's wrong?"

"I don't know."

"Are you happy?"

"Oh yes. Yes."

"Then why are you crying?"

"I don't know. Love me, Will. I don't know. Love me."

25

AROUND AND AROUND on this tower. Down that path in the evening and home again in the dark, following the way by starlight and memory. With pack on my back. Beast of burden. If only that were the only burden. What is this thing that haunts my soul night after night and day after day, week after month after year? Aye, what is it, lass? My bonnie, bonnie lass. Year after year. Absurd. For they're everywhere, multiplying like fruit flies. The very skin of the earth crawls and itches with them. Of all those billions why that one? Pathetic absurdity. Only because of all the ones you've known and loved she was the only one you could not keep? Aye, where is she? Where is she now? I see her dancing again in the candlelight, spinning across the room, her black skirt twirling around her. Hair flying, eyes shining, arms outstretched. On the wall the white skull of a horse. I see her slender bones broken on rock, bleached in the sun, lost in some impossible place where no man will ever walk. Where the horned lizard and the tarantula crawl, where the shadow of the black vulture cruises over the stone and sand and cactus. Perhaps she is not *down there*. Perhaps she is dancing again in the arms of a man she loves, loves more than she ever loved me. In the city. In what city? Where? Ballantine thinks I'm mad. Men have died and worms have eaten them but not for love. He says. Men do not bind their souls to what is not attainable, he says. All have said. Not in this century, nor in Buddha's. Hopeless desire, hopeless longing. Hope too long deferred. O sly slim shy dim fading shadow. O stay, thou art so fair. Thou art fair, thou art fair. Oh my love, I see thee everywhere. In the wild eyes of a doe. In the dove's song. In the secret places of the forest. Sun gleaming on grass. The new moon thin as a sliver of ice hanging in the glow on the west. The whispering leaves. O madness. Absurdity. Sick with love. Kiss me with the kisses of thy mouth. Let me hear thy voice, for sweet is thy voice. Thy countenance is comely. Three thousand years ago in another desert land. In another world. Unreal world. Words. World of words, thoughts, sensations: desire and remembrance. Unreal? Unreal as rock. There down south is the mountain that we climbed. Beyond the mountain is a canyon we explored, a place where we got drunk on sunflowers and kisses and swam naked under a marble ledge. And the river. Down by the river. All day long the soft roar of the rapids around the bend. Supper on the fire. Juniper smoke. The whistle of a thrasher. Music of canyon wrens tumbling through the air. Greed of my lust. Golden down on the surface of her body. As if I had never seen a girl before in all my years on earth. Sweet sickness. Swooning through the afternoon. Green-gold river, auburn hair, the honey of her tongue. For how the girl could talk. Me so wrapped in fascination I scarcely heard a word she said. What did I say in reply? As little as necessary. What did I say? Her delicate ear, that receptacle for lies. Who now is telling her lies? Who lies with her and upon her and beneath her now? What is it now that penetrates the marrow of her bones? What stabs her through to the heart? Where could she have gone? Look at them, licking my salt. When October comes I'll murder you, my darlings, and carry you away. You think your days are numberless, they are not. You think you will live forever, you will not. Even the forest will die. Lightning from my rifle will strike you dead. There is death in my glance, death in my love. What is it that slides invisibly among my thoughts? What transparent thread weaves my days together? Always at the corner of my eye, just beyond the focus of my vision, something moves, disappears when I turn toward it. Day after day. Kill your deer and get out of here. My ax will fell the slender aspens down the way. Close that road for the winter. What did I say? Close that road.

26 Darling Will,

Tonight you must come to me. I am preparing a private extravaganza for you. I have new surprises for you, my darling. Stuffed peppers will be as nothing compared to what I am fixing for you tonight. And I have found a bottle of old wine. And will be wearing my new black skirt with the red and gold bands that you like. Everything will be as you like it best. Who cares what the neighbors think? As you say, fuck thy neighbor. Only not tonight, tonight I am being selfish and want you all to myself. (Did I spell it correctly?) Tonight I will be thy neighbor. There will be music and I will show you what I learned at Goucher, you think they don't teach girls anything there, I'll show you. Did you know I took ballet? And tomorrow we'll go down to the mountains and climb them. You can't get out of it, I know you have the next two days off. So bring your Kelty.

What else? Well only this, my darling: *Ya-ha-la-ni, ch'indy begay.* I love you, son of the devil. Oh kiss me with the kisses of thy mouth, for thy kisses are sweeter than wine. I'll say!

Yo te amo, mi amor. How's my Spanish coming along, my love? *Mi chingadero, mi pendejo, mi gran cajones dulce.* I wonder if you're a good teacher or not, really. Some of the words you taught me I can't find in my dictionary. Anyway, come, or I'll fly around your cabin all night like a crazy bat.

—S.

27 In the morning.

Ah yes—in the morning. In the morning she was there, really there, curled up against his back spoon-fashion, warm and nude and sleek as satin, dead asleep. Carefully he eased himself out of the double bag, attempting not to disturb her. She sighed, her hand sliding over his hips, but did not awake. He stood for a moment beside the bed, gazing down at her fair blond body in admiration and wonder, covered her again, kissed her gently on the forehead and stepped outside.

The sky was clear, the sun about to rise, the air in motion, cold on his naked limbs. He stepped inside, put on a long coat and moccasins, went out again quietly—the girl still sleeping—and across the rain-soaked clearing to the tower. Up the stairways to the lookout. Mists rolled over the forest, shrouded the ridges in dense blankets of wool-like foam. Nowhere yet a sign of smoke.

Descending, he took the galvanized tub from the outside wall, filled it at the pump and bathed himself in the cold water while the first rays of the sun slanted into the clearing. Shivering, he rubbed himself dry with a big towel, doing a little dance in the sunlight. Naked, clean, his skin tingling, his blood burning, he re-entered the cabin.

She was still asleep. As softly as he could Gatlin rebuilt the fire in the stove, blew the kindling into flame and set the iron lids back in place. The fire began to hum. He filled the kettle with fresh water and put it over the heat.

The girl opened her eyes. "What are you doing?"

"Stay there," he said. "Breakfast ain't ready yet."

"I was dreaming."

"Go back to sleep."

She smiled, stretched, rolled over, buried her head beneath the cover. Long bright hair spread fanwise over the pillow.

He took his straight razor and the leather strop and the steel mirror outside, filled a basin, honed the blade and shaved, as he always did, with nothing but the razor, cold water and soap. Grinning at his dark face in the mirror while the words and tune of an old song, folk, traditional, American, dallied through his mind: "Oh, she jumped in bed and covered up her head and swore I could not find her. . . ."

He threw the basin of soapy water, gray with his short whiskers, toward the nearest deer. They leaped aside, stopped, stared at him in amazement.

Inside again, he filled the coffeepot, removed an inner ring of the stovelid, set the pot over the flames. Once more the girl stirred, opened her eyes and peeked at him over the edge of the sleeping bag.

"Let me fix breakfast for you," she said.

"Not yet."

"Why don't you put some clothes on? You must be freezing."

He laughed. "I'm coming back to bed for a while. Watch out." And he sprang onto the bed, slid into the bag, crushed her in his arms.

"Oh Will, you're like an animal."

"I am an animal. Roll over."

"No."

"Then I'll make you."

"No. What're you doing?"

"You'll see."

"I can't see anything. I can't even kiss you like this."

"Yes you can."

"What are you doing?"

"You'll see."

"It seems so . . . vulgar."
"It sure is. By *God* you have a nice ass."
"It's too big."
"Oh no it isn't. It's just right. You're built like a girl, my girl."
"Kiss me. Please kiss me."
"I'll kiss you. I'm going to kiss every square round inch of you, lassie my lass."
"Aren't you going to make breakfast?"
"We're going to have breakfast in bed, my bonnie lass, my pretty bird, my chickadee, my hummingbird."
"You're crazy."
"I'm insane."
"You're a monster."
"I'm the devil himself."
"Shouldn't you go to work?"
"Whenever you're ready."
"Oh Will, you're terrible."
"Duty calls."
"You're absolutely shameless."
"If only your mother could see you now."
"Oh Will . . ."
"Oh Sandy my darling . . ."
"Kiss me, Will, kiss me . . ."

The fire roared softly in the stove, the kettle sang, the water boiled away in the coffeepot. The mouse cowered in his nest beneath the cupboard while into the cabin, through the door left half ajar, came a pair of glossy chipmunks, quick and quivering as mercury, searching for their forgotten breakfast under the table. Bluejays and gray squirrels screeched, jabbered, quarreled in the trees outside, and the deer, as the sun rose up, faded away into the forest.

They sat at the table eating the breakfast which Gatlin, after all, had cooked. The eggs, the bacon thick as slices of ham, the biscuits and jam, the hot and smoking coffee.

"How strange it is," she said.

"What is?"

"Well, I'm not a virgin any more, am I?"

"I reckon not. I'd say not. More coffee?"

"Yes please. Did I . . ." She blushed, averting her face from his smiling gaze. "Did I bleed very much?"

"Not that I noticed. I doubt it."

"All that big issue over a little tissue. But it still hurts, a little. God Will, I can still feel you inside me. What a funny feeling. It aches somehow. It's wonderful."

"Yes it is."

"Even up here it hurts, a little. My breasts feel sort of swollen."

"Yes, you're beginning to bloom all over. You're becoming a woman now, MacKenzie."

"You mean . . . my breasts will get bigger?"

"All it takes is loving."

"I'm glad. My bust is too small."

"No it isn't. You're beautiful."

"Isn't it too small?"

"No. You're perfect. Finish your breakfast."

For a minute she was silent, eating. Then she said, "Well, now we've done it two different ways. How many different ways are there?"

He laughed. "Let me count." Mocking her, he squinted upward and began to enumerate the ways on his fingers.

"The girls at Goucher said that there are only five basic positions and that all the others are just variations on the five basic ones. Is that right? Technically speaking?"

"There's only one basic position. To be technical."

"Only one?"

"In love."

"You are a romantic, aren't you?"

"Yes."

She thought again for a minute or two. "Larry always swore that the girl he married would be a virgin."

Guess again, son, thought Gatlin. "Don't worry about that," he said aloud. "He'll never know the difference. Only technicians worry about things like that."

"What if I got pregnant?"

"I'd marry you. If he wouldn't."

"What if I didn't?"

"I'd marry you anyway."

Gatlin poured himself more coffee. Both he and the girl said nothing for some time.

"Are you proposing to me, Mr. Gatlin?"

"Sure." Drinking his coffee.

"You haven't even said that you love me."

He said nothing.

She said, "Well, you don't mind if I think it over for a while first, do you?"

"You go ahead." He lowered his cup and got to his feet. "Let's climb the tower."

"Right now?"

"I smell smoke."

"I'll clean up the dishes."

"The animals will clean them."

"The animals?"

He grinned at her. "When the coyotes refuse to eat off my plates I know it's time to wash them."

She started to protest but he hugged her close, silencing her with kisses. "Come on. Up the tower. I'll beat you to the top."

She tore loose from his arms, ran for the tower and started up the stairways. Gatlin climbed below her, lost in admiration, watching the sunlight shine through her thin yellow dress, loving her from every angle. Overnight he had become a millionaire, a king, a famous movie star, a saint with sex, immortal.

She stopped when she realized what he was doing and pulled her skirt tightly around her legs. "You filthy beast," she said. "You're unspeakable."

He came up slowly beside her, panting for breath. Kissed her earlobes and pressed her breasts in his hands. "Yes," he said.

"You're a sex maniac."

"Yes. And so are you."

"Depraved, dirty old man."

"Beautiful, I say."

"Disgusting, filthy-minded animal."

"Yes!"

He squeezed her small waist in his two big hands, bent her backward over the railing and smothered her protests with another kiss, a deep and prolonged and hungry kiss. Then released her and went on up into the lookout. Still no smoke. He reached for the microphone as Sandy entered.

"Seven eighty," he said, "seven eighty-one."

The dispatcher's voice crackled out of the speaker. "Morning, Will. How's she look up there today?"

His girl, *his girl,* stood across the room, tall and fair and slender and lovely, her face flushed and her wild hair shining, watching him across the sights of the firefinder.

"Wendell," said Gatlin, "I never saw a prettier sight in my life."

"Lot of lightning yesterday evening. See any smoke?"

"Not yet. All clear so far."

After a pause the dispatcher said, "You're about an hour late this morning, Will. Everything all right up there?"

"Wendell, old horse, everything is great up here."

"Sound like you're drunk."

"Worse. I'm in love."

"In love?"

"In love, Wendell, in love. I even love you this morning, Wendell, old horse."

"Okay Will, thanks. But don't forget this call might be monitored by the F.C.C."

"I'll tell the world."

"You already have. Seven eighty clear."

"Seven eighty-one. Alleluia. Alleluia."

She stared at him across the instruments, suppressing a giggle with her hand. "You'll lose your job."

"Job," he said, "what job? You call this a job? This is no job, this is play. Come here."

"What are you going to do?"

He sat on the high armless chair near the radiotelephone and beckoned to her. "Come here."

"What are you going to do?"

"Time for Lesson Number Three. Come." He held out his arms and smiled.

And she did.

28 Dear Willy,

Willy, old man, I've got it all figured out. How to get over this fixation of mine. This obsession of mine with you may remember what, though of course you no longer remember what it's like.

(I mean love, of course. No, I mean sex. With a capital X.)

What are the elements of the situation, the basic building stones of this gigantic edifice of misery and frustration and drunkenness we call Modern Life? I take it they are three, namely (1) sex, (2) love, and (3) marriage. Now consider the possible combinations of these three fundamental elements:

1) sex (without love or marriage)
2) love (without sex or marriage)
3) marriage (without love or sex)
4) sex and love (without marriage)
5) sex and marriage (without love)
6) love and marriage (without sex—more common than is commonly supposed)
7) sex and love and marriage (the utopian dream, good in theory but unworkable in practice, e.g., like the profit system)

These are the seven and the only possible seven combinations. Now, given this premise, which of the seven is most likely to enable me to overcome my obsession? I proceed without syllogizing to my conclusion:

The only way to conquer sex is to surrender to it. Sex is the only possible answer to our sexual problem.

That much understood, we advance to the formulation of my panacea, or what I like to call "A Modest Proposal for the Immediate Moral Improvement of These United States, or, The Virtues and Benefits of Universal Sexual Prostitution Justly Observed: The Whorehouse as Community Social Center, Cementer of Family Life (i.e., The Family That Whores Together Snores Together) and Inspirational Exemplar for the Young."

It is not enough simply to legalize prostitution. We must make it honorific. The whore, like the physician, the psychiatrist, the teacher, the artist (and as you know, a good whore is a composite of all of these) should be a respected member of the community. The most venerable of professions deserves also to be the most venerated.

Next, as to the physical facilities. I envision each town or commune within a city as having its own public whorehouse, a large and beautiful building erected at public expense, designed and decorated by the best of local architects and sculptors, and so placed within the community as to be the cynosure of every eye, the apex of every thoroughfare, the pride and delight of every citizen.

Now as to staffing. There is no reason whatsoever why we must rely on the archaic system of the penal-type brothel, where the girls are recruited from outside the community and shut up like lepers within the house until, worn out with abuse and overuse, they are cast out into the streets. No, our model whorehouse—and let us now call it what I actually have in mind, our Holy Temple of Eros—will be open to all girls, all women, of any age, background, race or creed or dimensions who think they have something to offer that men, some men, or at least one man might desire. Our girls will not be expected to live in the Temple but will be perfectly free to come and go as they wish, to set whatever fee they may wish on their services, and to keep all of their earnings, without exception.

The part-time worker and the amateur, while not freely encouraged, will be permitted to work within the Temple. It is not beyond the bounds of reason that certain husbands and wives, coming secretly and separately, might rediscover and re-evaluate one another on these occasions, thus salvaging many a marriage that seemed headed for the rocks.

Need I point out that I see my utopian whorehouse as the salvation of the institution of marriage in our America? The courtesan as not the enemy but the dearest friend of wife and matrimony? Because the typical husband, bored with his wife, will no longer have to engage in furtive love affairs with secretaries and waitresses in order to satisfy his legitimate need for novelty; instead he merely strolls down to the community social center, arm in arm with his friends, spends a pleasant evening at the club and returns home the same night to a wife and children whose charms and virtues he is now more ready to appreciate. With sex removed from its current place as the engine of marriage—a role which sex is not powerful or enduring enough to long serve—then the true purpose of marriage will be restored: namely, the breeding and rearing of children.

And what about romantic love? This: if romantic love has any genuine value it will not be destroyed by cheap and easy sex. And if it has no such value then is it not high time we got rid of it once and for all? We bear too many psychic burdens already; if we were freed of romantic love, freed at the same time from this obsession with sex caused by continual temptation and insufficient satisfaction, we would all be happier, freer, healthier citizens, ready to face our daily chores with willing hearts and steady hands and clear, untroubled minds. No more pornography, no more sadistic rapes and murders, no more broken homes, and—who knows?—perhaps even no more wars.

Meanwhile, back to reality. Summer session almost over and they've given me a contract for the fall and winter terms. I guess I'll sign, what else can I do? Besides I like this town, and as you know, I love these California girls.

Darnelle has returned but I doubt if she'll stay, God bless her. Ah Willy, old comrade, she wants what every woman wants and needs and deserves, a little nest of her own, a place to hatch her brood, a good provider to bring home the worms. In a word, she wants me. Me, Willy. And how can I go through all that again? How can I do it all again? I don't know, Willy, I really don't know. It's too much for one man to understand. I believe in marriage, Willy, I actually believe in marriage. But I can't quite face it all again. And I must tell her so. But how?

Write, you bastard. Is it useless to beg you to write? I know you're alive, I can hear you breathing out there in the night, in the dark of your forest, counting the stars, counting the leaves on the aspens.

Maybe I'll come and see you for a few days in the fall. Someone's got to look after you before you hurt yourself. Besides, and I'll confess it, there are times, few but true, when I think that you might be right after all. Withdraw from this madness and confusion, retreat to the forest, observe the frenzied strivings and suicidal passions of our fellow men with compassion, humor and understanding —but, from a safe distance.

Anyway, so much for now. Best regards from your most humble and obedient servant,

—Red Dog Ballantine, Ph.D.

29

HER HEAD on his arm, her eyes closed. The dark lashes against the suntanned cheek. With a finger he traced the slight high bridge of her nose, the defile of her parted lips. Those strong little teeth, not quite straight, so clean and white as to be almost translucent. His moving forefinger proceeded down the profile of her chin and throat and across the brown skin of her chest into the fragrant cleft between her breasts. My growing girl. Her relaxed nipples, sweet as cinnamon. Down the tender swale of her belly into the curly light brown thicket of her pubic hair. Delicately, very delicately, not wishing to awaken her, down the velvet crease of her sex and into the long brown valley between her closed thighs, softly over that nearly invisible, intangible down, bleached golden by the sun, to the rounded gloss of her knees. He let his hand come to rest there, kissed the freckles on her shoulder, the dark mole, the rich tangle of her wet dark hair, smelling of the water, glinting like copper.

She stirred, sighed.

"Sleep," he whispered, "dream . . . sleep"—and relaxed again—"sleep . . ."

Under the ledge of rock the green dark water lay, a deep pool with hidden currents. On the far side, beyond a stand of tufted cane, stood sycamore trees with smooth boles of milk-white and brown; the sunlight of late afternoon broke and lost itself within the multitude of leaves. Among those leaves only minutes earlier he had seen the face of a green god, goat-horned, smiling on their delirium.

Scarlet dragonflies struck across the pool. The ripple spread concentric waves. Flies, bees, cicada droned in the amber light among the reeds. Upstream, on the hard sand, the killdeer cried. Ravens. In the stillness came a sound like a distant cough.

In the silence.

30

They were the first to ride the lift that morning, and as they rose without effort through the mountain air above treetops toward the crags above timberline, they held each other tightly, and kissed, and looked down between their dangling feet at the rocks passing below.

"Some mountain climb," she said.

"You'll see."

"So this is how you climb mountains? In a chairlift."
"You'll see." And he sang for her.

> "O'Malley is dead and O'Grady don't know it,
> O'Grady is dead and O'Malley don't know it,
> They're both of 'em dead and in the same bed
> And neither one knows that the other one's dead."

"How touching."
"How about this?"

> "Green grow the rashes O,
> Green grow the rashes O,
> The sweetest bed I ever knew
> Was the bellies o' the lasses O!"

"You're so romantic, Mr. Gatlin."
"Okay, you don't like that one either. Let me see. Have you heard this one? 'I know she's a coal miner's daughter, because she's got slack in her pants.'"
"Your voice does carry well, Mr. Gatlin. I am sure they can hear you all the way down to the city."
"Okay, a gentle song, *poco piano:*

> "The workers' flag is deepest red,
> It shrouded oft our martyred dead,
> But ere their limbs grew stiff and cold,
> Their lifeblood dyed its every fold."

"Some *piano*. I'll bet they can hear you all the way to Washington."

"All right. Let's listen to the mountains."

Wordlessly, silently, they floated skyward, above the pine and spruce and fir and aspen toward the bleak black volcanic rocks of the peak. Kissing like doves, embracing, caressing, careless and reckless, tumbling from the lift and falling, falling through silken clouds.

"Watch your step, folks."

And there was a boy in the wooden shack at the top of the line, calling to them, a pimply adolescent with adam's apple, undescended testicles (he knew the type) and bright blue bored eyes peeping at them through sun-bleached bangs. From the joy in his heart Gatlin gave the nice punk kid a shiny new U.S. Government copper quarter.

"For you, son."

"Thanks, sir. Last trip down at four o'clock, sir," he said, leering at Sandy.

"We're not coming back," she said, and they both laughed at the surprise on the boy's face.

They scrambled up the rocks, through the alpine shrubbery to the summit of the first peak, where they stopped to rest and consider new angles on the world from this imperial height. They were already above the few scattered clouds in the morning sky.

Kissing her again, he passed his hand up her bare brown legs, stroking the marvelous surface of her thigh. But she held his hand when it came too near.

"No," she said, blowing on his ear, "no sex on mountain climbs. That's the rule."

"Who made that rule?"

"You did."

"I suspend the rule."

She picked a miniature mountain violet and stuck it in the buttonhole of his lapel. "There. Take that instead."

"Not enough."

"Give me something to eat," she said.

"Here."

"No, not that. Oh, you evil man. You disgusting beast. Food, I mean."

"Is this not food? You've taken twenty pounds out of me in a month. You're getting sleek and fat, MacKenzie, off my very life's essence. Reducing me to a poor pale shriveled husk of me former self."

"Clown." She pulled at the rucksack on his back, tugged it off, opened it and drew out bread, cheese, chocolate, shelled nuts, jerky, oranges, a canteen. "You've got a feast in here."

"Enough." He opened the canteen and drank deeply, head back, eyes closed against the blazing white sun. As always, the thin air and the dazzling light of the peaks gave him a brilliant thirst.

The girl asked for water. He gave her water. They ate a little, repacked the bag, and went on, down from this first point toward a ridge that led to the highest summit of the range, three miles beyond. On the fine edge of the ridge they looked down on their left to the winter ski slopes, on their right into the collapsed caldera of what had once been a great volcano. Farther out, in all directions, the desert plain lay studded with cinder cones, the warts and knobs of old eruptions, and rigid death-black lava flows.

"Are they all dead now?"

"Dormant," he said. "Only sleeping. May they rest in peace till we get down from here."

They walked over the gray rock daubed with green, red, yellow, rust-brown lichens, past the twisted and silvery skeletons of long-dead trees, and along an icy cornice of snow which overhung the inner basin. Down in there, among the rock slides, snow fields and pinnacles, were islands of forest, and springs and running streams, deer and columbines and purple fields of lupine and larkspur. Above them was only the sun, the solitary star in a burning wine-dark sky. In the saddle of the ridge, where an ancient trail came up from below, they found a cairn of stones. He added a stone to the cairn. She did the same.

"For good luck," he said.

"For you," she said.

Here the wind was blowing. As they walked on he sang in the teeth of it, bellowing back.

> "Then raise the scarlet banner high,
> Beneath its folds we'll live or die;
> Though cowards flinch and traitors sneer,
> We'll keep the red flag flying here!"

"My but you're feeling cocky this morning."

"That's the word, lass."

> "Eyes like the morning star,
> Lips like a rose,
> Sandy she's a pretty girl,
> God almighty knows."

"I like that one better. It's not so warlike."

He pulled her close. "Do you realize that we haven't kissed for"—he glanced at the sun—"for fifteen minutes? We're losing time, losing time, the sun is racing for the west." He kissed her, they kissed, lips parted, tongue on tongue. Eyes half open, he could see the infinitely fine blue veins of her closed eyelids, her coal-black lashes, a tangle of the bronze hair. The magic of her body in his arms, so firm, warm, vibrant with life. Now, he thought, let them strike us dead if they must, it matters no more now, they can take nothing from us.

The ridge ascended toward the highest peak. Halfway there, close to noon, they sought shelter from the piercing wind in a cove among the boulders, warm with sunlight.

On a tiny ledge they sat side by side, legs hanging over the brink of a five-hundred-foot drop.

"You're not afraid of heights, are you?" he said.

"I love them."

"How about heights of passion?"

"Anything high and good." She was opening his rucksack again, bringing out the food.

"Good. Give me bread. Give me water. Give me the honey of thy tongue. You know what, Sandy?"

"What?"

"Let's fuck."

"Are you crazy? Here?"

"Right here, on top of the mountain, with the whole damned world looking on. And then we'll lie back and listen to the applause. There'll be a standing ovation. We'll—"

"You're out of your mind. We'd fall off. Besides . . . I don't really like that word."

"Word? You don't like the word?" He stared at her as she unwrapped the cheese and sliced thick chunks from her homemade bread. "What shall we say? Sexual intercourse? Shall we commit sexual intercourse?"

"It does sound clinical. I mean criminal."

"How about inner course? Well, we could have conjugal relations."

"That's ridiculous."

"Yes it is. Okay, suppose we have carnal knowledge of each other."

"Ridiculous."

"How about sexual congress?"

"Sounds like a convention. Here. Eat. Shut up."

"Intimate relations?"

"That makes me think of Mother and Dad. Would you unscrew the canteen cap, please?"

"There's the word. No, it's no good. Maybe it's all in

the spelling." He opened the canteen and handed it to her. "Suppose we spelled it with a ph, maybe that would sound more genteel. Shall we p-h-u-c-k, my dear? Or, I say, we could give it a bit of an English twist, spell it p-h-u-q-u-e, what? I say, young lady, would you care for a bit of phuquing now, don't you know? Oh Jeeves, would you hold my hat for a moment, there's a good chap."

"Oh shut up." She laughed at him, her mouth full of bread and cheese. "Want some water?"

"Of course we could always simply make love."

"That's best."

"But vague. Not quite exact."

"You're beginning to sound like a professor, Mr. Gatlin."

"A pedant, you mean."

"Yes. How about an orange?"

"Yes. You're lovely, MacKenzie."

"Keep saying that and I'll begin to believe it."

"When you believe it you'll be twice as lovely as you are now."

Eating slowly, they stared out over the vast gulf of the crater, over the foothills, out at the desert and the world's curving rim.

"Which do you like best," she said, "mountains or desert?"

"Making love to you."

"That wasn't my question. Mountains or desert?"

"I feel at home in the mountains," he said. "I understand the forest. Trees are human."

"Then you don't like the desert."

"There's something about the desert I don't understand. Something out there, in that emptiness, frightens me a little."

"And the canyon?"

"The canyon? Yes, the canyon. The underworld. The

Hopis think it's the home of evil spirits. They may be right."

"I like it."

"You're braver than I am, lass. We get timid in our middle age."

They both fell silent for a few moments.

"We'd better get on," he said. "Still a long way to go and we haven't even conquered the summit yet. They repacked the bag, he shouldered it onto his back. She started ahead. "One moment," he said, and cornered her against the rock. He slipped a hand under her sweater. "Two of them," he said, marveling. "Let's get one out where I can kiss it. For good luck. Either one will do."

"Oh Will, come on."

"Either one." Closing her eyes, she submitted to his fondling. And after a time he said, "There. Now. Now we can go."

"You're crazy," she said.

"Yes," he said, "isn't it lucky!"

An hour later they reached the peak, where a demon wind howled in their faces, tore at their hair, whipped the girl's kilt about her legs. Gatlin unknotted the red bandana from around his neck and held it high, like a flag.

"*Venceremos! No pasaran!* Let all the pissing conduits be filled with claret wine!"

"Communist!" she shouted, laughing in the blast of the wind, her eyes exalted, holding him around the waist to keep from being swept away. "Anarchist!"

"Worse than that!" he shouted back. "A lover! A lover!"

Here too was a cairn of stones and among the stones a steel canister containing a pencil and tablet, on which they left their autograph in archaic Spanish: *"Pasemos por aqui,* Sandra MacKenzie *y* William Gatlin, *amadors."*

And then, fighting the wind, like forcing a way through

an invisible wall, they descended the ridge beyond, where there was no trail, and entered the inner basin of the mountain. Free of the wind, they picked their way down a talus of loose rock between towering extrusions of ancient lava—shapes like gargoyles, helmeted warriors, fin-backed tyrannosaurs in various hues of rust and sulfurous yellow, painted with lichens—until they came again to the order and sanity of the forest, the scented pines, the slim and virginal aspens, and grassy fields glowing with silverleaf lupine, larkspur, scarlet pentstemon, where small butterflies with yellow wings, like flying flowers, danced in the air and sunlight.

They lay on the warm grass, resting, listening to the wind pour with the sound of many rivers through the trees, till desire rose like fever and drunkenness in their nerves, their blood, their bodies, between them, conjoining them in a roaring flood of love and lust and generosity.

"I saw blue," she said.
"Blue what?"
"I don't know. Just blue."
"The sky."
"No. How could I see the sky with you all over me? It was more like . . . blue lightning. Sheets of it."
"A vision."
"Fission. Nuclear fission."
"Fusion."
"Yes. Oh, I can feel you getting smaller and smaller. Don't go, please don't go."
"I don't want to go. But you're squeezing me out."
"I can't help it. I'm trying to keep you in."
"Lie still. Be quiet."
"There's an ant crawling up my leg."
"I'll get him. There he goes." He rolled over, pulling her on top of him. "What God hath joined let no ant put asunder. Well."

"Now you did it."

"Well."

She drew somewhat aside, examining his body, exploring it with her hand, fondling his penis. "How strange a man is. Poor limp helpless little thing, what good are you now?"

"I am the resurrection and the life."

"I want to see it resurrect. Make it stand up."

"Thy rod and thy staff they comfort me. *You* make it stand up, it has a mind of its own. I can't do it."

"All right, I'll do it." She bent over him.

"No, wait a minute. Or about a week. I'm dead, lass. We still have five or six miles to go. Have mercy on your old man. Here, lie still, put your head on my arm."

"Where's your knife?"

"Very well, okay, cut it off. Take it home and get it stuffed and mounted, hang it on the wall. Memento mori, till the world cracks and all the cows come home." He turned on his side, closing his eyes. Felt her putting flowers in his hair, heard her walking softly away, singing. He dozed, naked in the sun.

Minutes later—hours later?—he awoke, sat up. At first he thought he was alone and the shock of it was like a blow on the heart. And then he saw her only fifty feet away in the spangled light and shade of an aspen, nude as an angel, sucking at her finger and scratching on the bark of the tree with his knife. He got up, went to her.

"What are you doing?"

"Cut my finger. This knife is sharp."

"Of course it's sharp. Let me finish this for you." Gently, he took the knife from her hand and completed the inscription she had begun, the valentine heart, the initial letters of their names. "Sentimentalist. Vandal."

"I know. This is something I always wanted to do."

He folded the knife in his hand and draped an arm

around her waist. "Something I've always wanted to do too. Come here." He led her back into the sunshine, stooped and picked some flowers. He put one in her hair, one in her mouth, one in her pubic hair. There were two left, mountain violets with short thick stems. She stared at him, smiling. He grinned.

"Bend over," he said.

She backed away. "Oh no you don't. Pervert. Vulgar pervert."

"Why not?" he said. "Then I'll pluck them out with my teeth. What's wrong with that?"

"You're disgusting." Giggling, she tried to turn and run but he held her, wrestled with her, threw her to the grass. Strong and quick, she resisted for a little while, holding him off with averted face, locked knees, stiff and struggling arms. Then suddenly softened and surrendered to him, opening herself for him like a flower in the sun, moaning with pleasure.

"Will, oh Will, do it to me now."

"I've got you, lass." He entered into her. "Now what?"

"What?"

"What do we do now?"

"I don't know."

"Well, think of something."

"The flowers. Do it."

"Flowers. What flowers?"

"Do it to me."

But they, while the sun ran, became themselves a kind of flower and sank into a great white blue-veined flower that blinded thought and every sense with its dazzling, overwhelming, perfumed and momentary splendor. That is what they knew.

And went on, later.

In a glade near the bottom of a ravine they found banks

of yellow columbines. A little farther and they found one solitary blue columbine, loveliest and rarest of mountain flowers, beside a brook. Clear cold water flowed in rills over the rock and moss. He knelt, refilled the canteen, passed one hand up the back of her thigh, kissed her knees. She stared at something upstream.

"What's that?"

He looked where she was pointing and saw a dark shapeless thing that appeared to be alive, moving slowly over the stream bed.

"What is it?"

"I don't know," he said, still on his knees.

They watched. The shapeless thing took on a shape, became a pair of wings and a beaked head and a pair of clawed feet, a great bird that stepped toward them and launched itself into the air with heavy, powerful wing strokes, rising slowly, bearing straight toward them not ten feet off the ground. Gatlin stood up quickly, raising his arms. The bird passed close above their heads, wings thundering, gained momentum and rose toward the cliffs.

"Golden eagle," the girl said.

Gatlin stared at the bird rising higher and higher into the air. "A good omen."

"I thought you didn't believe in omens."

"I believe in *good* omens," he said.

"But not in bad omens."

"Naturally not."

"Is that fair?"

"It's prudent. Call me prudence. Let's go."

"Okay, Prudence."

He picked her up and carried her across the little stream, set her down, his hand lingering on her round rear.

"You're rather free with your hands, sir."

"There's no charge."

"We'll never get home if you keep this up."

"By God, Sandy, you're right." He paused for a moment, gazing into the forest. They were now in an open park of tall yellow pine, naves full of sunshine and golden motes of dust leading before them.

"I wonder if you even know where we are," she said.

He smiled. "I know where we should be. So we're not lost."

She looked up at him, kissed him, drew back. "You should smile more often. You're beautiful when you smile. And so formidable when you frown."

"Well," he said. "Okay."

She picked a flower, stuck it in his hair. He picked another and threaded the stem of it through a buttonhole of his fly.

"How unspeakable you are."

"Kiss my flower."

"I will not."

"Let's follow the flower then."

With a glance at the sun, now sinking into the treetops, he started off, the girl at his side. They came to a track in the forest, parallel wagon ruts which brought them, after another mile, to the edge of open country. Below was a road and up the road, not far, they could see the buildings of the ski lodge, the glimmer of moving cars in dust and evening light.

As they climbed the steps of the restaurant, tired and hungry, thirsty and happy and disheveled, she reminded him of the wilted flowers that dangled from his ears, his teeth, his pants, his boots, his backpack. He grinned, eying the flowers in Sandy's hair, drew her hard against his side and marched into the doorway.

"We'll spread the word," he said.

PART III

In the Evening

31 DEAR WILL,

Thanks for the check. It came just in time. Consuela fell off her bike a few days ago. She broke a front tooth. The dentist charged me $50 to cap it. This was her second tooth. Consuela is eight years old now. Would you believe it?

But of course you don't come down to see us for a long time. Almost a year now. The children would like to see you sometime. They like you very much. (God knows they like you more than they ever did their father. If they never see him again it's too soon for me.) They like your presents very much. They ask me about you all the time.

Will, I know you don't really love me. I know you don't want to marry me. Just the same I would like to see you now and then. Like we used to. They were good times. I miss you, Will. The kids miss you too.

Well I'm still working at the cafeteria. It is a lousy job as you know but what else can I do.

The kids are doing good in school. Consuela is very bright. She gets almost all A's every time. She talks about you a lot.

Please come and visit us. If you can't come write us a letter more often. We all love to hear from you. You know that, Will. Call me on the phone now and then. You know the number.

      Sincerely yours,
      your Rosalie

32

THE IDIOT. Alone on tower. Walking around the catwalk. Again. And again. And again. Leaning on the rail to stare at the respiring forest, to hear from the radio antennas on the roof the mystic music—like distant bugle calls, like ancient horns: *Roland! Oliver! Siegfried! Cuauhtemoc! Hamilcar! Leonidas! Joshua! Gilgamesh!*—back and back into time more remote than human memory. But thinking of her voice, the gentleness of her hands, her wild hair, her eyes in firelight. To watch the clouds flaring with lightning (blue lightning!) and hear the barrage of rolling thunder. To look down, down at the clearing ninety feet below, where the old cabin shakes, creaks and groans in the wind, where scuds of pine duff and dust spin across the web of his many pathways, his ruts in the soil of the earth.

Now he would welcome fire, the crash of a bolt spiraling down a tree trunk, the rip of a fireball through the forest carpet, even the hurricane roar and onrush of a great crown fire. Anything, anything, to smash his idleness and reverie, to drag him into the midst of trouble and terror.

In the evening. The tower quivers before the wind, storm clouds overspread the plateau, obscure the rim of the canyon, blot out the far-off mountains. Lightning crackles from cloud to cloud, cleaving the sky with a noise like the crack of doom. The air is electrified. As he descends the stairs in the dark, in his solitude, a bluish light, St. Elmo's fire, glows on the girders, on the railings, on the aerial and lightning rod, shining in the gloom with eerie corposant points of flame. Tower and forest and world—ship without stars, in a boundless sea— sail into night.

He sings.

> "The moon's my constant mistress,
> The lonely owl my morrow,
> The flaming drake and the night-crow make
> Me music to my sorrow."

33

WHEN HE CAME OUT of the dining room of the lodge and started down the steps in front and saw a young man standing there, on the walk, facing him, waiting for him, he knew at once what it meant.

People were moving by. Tourists, families with children, college girls on summer vacation. Someone carried a transistor radio from which, fading away, he heard the sounds of music. He could even hear the words, something about a fair, but did not recognize the song.

Although it was a warm evening, warm at least for the high country, this young man was pulling on fur-lined leather dress gloves as Gatlin approached him. Except for the gloves his clothing was conventional: light slacks, a dark blue blazer with the crest of some prep school on the breast pocket, sport shirt, a scarf. Conventional, expensive, informal.

The young man was not quite as tall as Gatlin but well formed, athletic, suggesting even in his waiting stance a fine sense of balance and poise and alertness. His short blond hair was brushed to a high gloss, his skin glowed, his eyes—bold, darkly violet, beautiful as a girl's—glittered with reflected light and with something else, a controlled fury, an intensity of carefully measured rage, that transformed an otherwise pleasing face into the semblance of rigid anger, exalted despair.

"Mr. Gatlin."

Gatlin halted. "Yes."

"Maybe you know who I am."

"You must be Larry."

A man and woman passed cautiously between them, abruptly silent. Others came out of the Lodge.

The young man nodded toward the darkness of the parking lot, beyond the range of the lights. "Shall we go over there?"

"All right."

They walked side by side the short distance to the lot, not speaking. Gatlin was aware of the stiffness in his companion's breathing, as if he were constricted about the chest. For himself, in himself, he felt only a passive resignation toward an event which he had long expected, for which he had no plan, no defense; he was painfully conscious of the other's pain.

They stopped in the shadows, half facing each other.

"Now. Tell me. Where is she?"

Gatlin paused. "I don't know."

"What have you done with her?"

Gatlin said nothing.

"Where did she go?"

"I'm sorry," Gatlin said. "I don't know."

"You knew she was gone."

He sighed. "She told me she wanted to go somewhere for a few days, to be alone. She didn't seem to know then where she would go."

"This is what she told you?"

"I didn't see her. She left me . . . a note."

"She left you a note." In the darkness the young man echoed Gatlin's sigh. After a moment he said, "When will she be back?"

"I don't know. I thought she might be back now. I was going over there, to her place, when I saw you."

"She's not home, Mr. Gatlin."

He said nothing.

"She's not home, Mr. Gatlin," Larry repeated, his voice rising. "Where is she?"

"Well, I told you—"

"I want to know what you've done with her, Mr. Gatlin."

"What do you mean?"

"You. You. You're a goddamned lying swine, Mr. Gatlin."

Wearily he shrugged, making no reply.

"You're contemptible, Mr. Gatlin. You are scum."

Wearily he waited, saying, "I've done Sandy no harm. I even think I might have made her happy, for a while."

The other stared at him, astounded, outraged. "No harm? No harm? Made her happy? Why, you damned rotten corrupt . . . My God, you had no right to her whatever. You had no right to even . . . speak to her."

"That's for Sandy to decide."

"Is it? Oh is it? We were engaged, Mr. Gatlin. She loved me. We were going to get married this fall. And then you, you rotten scum, you . . . What are you anyway? What kind of a man are you?"

He did not answer. Hands in his pockets, staring at the trees, waiting, Gatlin said nothing.

The young man made a harsh choking sound, a kind of laugh. He held up his gloved hands, clenched. "I was going to knock your goddamned teeth down your goddamned throat, Mr. Gatlin. But now. Christ, I didn't guess you'd be a coward too. Now I'd be ashamed to touch you with a stick."

Gatlin sighed. The night was getting on, he was tired, dejected, tired of waiting. He had hoped to be spending the night with the girl. Not with this inspired bore. "Keep your flaps up, flyboy," he said.

Suddenly the other tensed. "What was that? You . . . ?"

"A man takes care of his own," Gatlin said.

"Ah, why you son of a bitch!"

And he swung, the leather-gloved fist smashed into Gatlin's face, rocking him backward. Now the young man advanced expertly—this was what he was trained for, what he wanted—and punched Gatlin in the belly, again in the face, forcing him back against the fender of a parked car. Dazed, shocked, relieved, Gatlin held his hands before his face and waited for the next blow. He was a little surprised to find himself still on his feet, still aware.

"You bastard. Won't you fight?" The young man hesitated, his fists ready, his body balanced, waiting for Gatlin to make a move. "Are you really a coward?"

Slumped against the car, Gatlin touched the bruises on his face. He could feel and taste the warm salty blood beginning to flow inside his cheek. "I'd rather buy you a drink," he said, grinning crookedly. "And one for myself."

Larry lowered his fists. "You can go to hell."

"I think—"

"Go to hell."

"I think maybe," Gatlin said, and stopped, straining for a deep breath. The blow in the stomach was making him sick. "I think"—he tried again—"that maybe we ought to try to find out where . . ."

"What?"

"Where . . ."

"Can't you talk?"

"Where . . ."

And then he saw his companion, his rival, disappearing into a fog, a mist that came from nowhere, from everywhere, and heard his voice becoming remote and dim and very small, and Gatlin realized, faintly, humorously, that if he didn't lower himself to the ground he was going to fall. And fall through a distance that was very great, becoming each moment much greater.

34

IN HIS POCKET, the cool circlet of silver. Cold silver, like the gleam of moonlight on water. He fingered it, over and over, in his pocket, as they talked, knowing it would enclose her slender wrist as easily as his hand enclasped her ankle, as naturally as his hand might lift and cup her breast.

"He's coming?"

"Next week."

"Did I tell you he wrote me a letter once, about a month ago?"

"*He* told me. You never answered him."

"I'm not a good letter writer."

"Don't I know that. Your letters to me. In our log. One word. *Venez.* Or *venga.* Or *venite.*"

"Or come."

"Or come. Nothing but commands. Never a tender word of love. I wonder if you really love me. For all your antics and crazy songs and wild places and crazy ways to make love . . . you've never really said, not once, that you love me."

He sang his new song.

> "She was the lovely stranger
> who married a forest ranger
> a dog and a duck
> and never was seen again."

"Some proposal. That's your proposal to me?"

"Call it whatever you want."

"Sounds more like a proposition to me, Mr. Gatlin."

"I want you to come with me and stay with me for the rest of my life. If I live that long."

"Live in a shack in the woods for the rest of my life, eating poached deer?"

"Yes."

"Raise my children in a treehouse?"

He was silent.

"Do you know that Larry's been calling me every night? *Every night.* And writing to me almost every day. He really needs me, Will. Not like you. He really needs me and really wants me. He always has, or almost always."

He said nothing. The words he was meant to say remained locked in his head. *I love you,* and so forth. *Will you marry me, Miss MacKenzie,* and so on. *I am yours forever, beloved, through all eternity,* and what not. He could not quite get them out.

"He'd do anything for me, Will. He's only a boy but he really loves me."

Really? he thought. He said nothing, although the words which he knew very well she needed to hear were right there, in his brain, resounding through the circuits of his nerves. *I too. Anything. Anything. Die for you. Go back to the schools again. Profess. Die. Live. Work for you, my love, my darling, my heart,* and so forth, in that vein. *Go back to the world again, back to the cities, emerge at last from this miserable pack rat's nest I've made in the forest.* Thusly, in that manner. The words were there, present. He had only to speak them. Presently, perhaps, he could find voice to utter.

"Aren't you going to say anything?"

He felt the bracelet in his jacket pocket, turning it around and around and around.

"Well?" She stared at him across her table. The flowers, the glowing new candles in old wine bottles, the remains of her latest "extravaganza." *Lasagna . . . lasagna!* This girl could do anything, anything. Bake bread. Scale a cliff. Dance on the tip of his finger. Rub his back, wash his hair, touch him with delicate intimacy in the most intimate, delicate places. Conjure the heart out of an oak, charm a rattlesnake into bliss. Did he love her? He loved the scent of her bare feet on the steps of his tower. He loved the edge of her skirt, the hem of her shadow, the sound of her voice within music. The anticipation of her smile. The slightly misaligned little front teeth. The mole on her shoulder, the dimples at the base of her spine, the golden down on the nape of her neck, the words that came out of her mind and mouth. "If only you would say something. Am I supposed to be a mind reader?"

He did not speak. In the air, surrounding, embracing, assuming them, floated a sweet, melancholy music. Sounds of a dying century, infinitely tender and subtle. Lost.

"I want you to need me," she said.
"I want you."
"Then why don't you say so?"
Lost. Lost.

35

AT THE RAIL, on the bridge of his ship, he races with the sun. Which, rising far behind, passes far above with the speed of a meteor, and blinds him as it descends before his eyes into the enameled clouds of fire, the seas of fascinating brilliance in the west, so vast and open, deep and fathomless.

That yawning abyss which makes us think of sleep.
He turns this way. That way. This way.
Now it is evening; now it is night.

In the cabin at midnight, by the soft light of the lantern, he writes the letters which he should have written years before. Burns them. The fire mutters in the stove, the wind pours through the forest outside, moaning in the pine trees, shaking the dry dead yellow leaves of the aspens. The sound of many rivers. The sound of falls. The sound of human voices. Under the old moon deer pass like phantoms through the clearing. Dead limbs of a pine grate against one another, the noise like a groan of pain, and the deer pause for a moment to listen.

36 Darling Will,

Darling, I don't think I'll be able to come this evening. What I really mean is I just *can't* come tonight. And the reason is I just have to get away by myself for a few days, try to think things through and figure things out. Larry will be here Sunday and I must decide exactly what I'm going to tell him. And how. You know what I mean.

Sweetheart Will, whatever happens, I love you. I will always love you. You and the forest and mountains are part of my life now and always will be.

Please don't be hurt by my not coming this one time. I am sure you understand how terrible this situation is for me and how important it is that I make absolutely certain I am doing the right thing for once in my life. After this I don't want to hurt anyone ever again.

If only you could help me a little more But I guess what you want is that I settle this thing myself, on my own, and no doubt that is the best way and the only way to do it.

I love you, darling. I love you, more than you know.

God I hope you find this note. You must. See you soon, I hope. Be patient with me.

Ya-ha-la-ni, ch'indy begay,
—S.

37

EARLY IN THE MORNING, before sunrise, he started down the trail into the canyon. At the head of this trail, near the end of the dirt road, her car had been seen three days earlier by one of the rangers, before the car too had disappeared.

Alone, the pack frame on his back, in the pack enough dehydrated food for ten days, enough water for two days. He would find more water, he hoped, distill it from the earth if necessary, go clear down to the river if he had to. Despite the August sun, the heat of the inferno, water seemed—*for him*—a lesser problem now.

"Look," Wendell had said, "they don't need you. We do."

"I'll be back."

"Who's gonna man the tower?"

"Put somebody else up there."

"I ain't got anybody else."

"Take it yourself."

"You're crazy. You're kidding. We got three fires going right now. You can't run out on us now, the whole goddamned forest will burn."

"Let it burn."

"Look," Wendell said, "I understand how you feel. But you're going about it the wrong way. They had a crew up and down that trail twice since the storm. They've gone through the canyon with helicopters and planes every day. The boatmen been all the way through on the river and ain't seen a thing. Besides, the girl isn't even in the canyon."

"You're sure about that, eh?"

"Well, god damn it, Will, her car is gone. She sure as hell didn't take the car down in the canyon."

"Maybe somebody stole the car."

"That don't mean a thing. She could be anywhere in the world now. Maybe she went home."

"She didn't."

"Maybe she went to the mountains."

"I'm going there next."

"She might be on her way back here right now."

"Maybe."

"Wherever she went, she sure as hell didn't go down in the canyon. Nobody would go down in there now. Not in August."

"She would. I'll see you."

"When you coming back?"

"In a week. Two weeks."

"They'll be hunting you next."

"Tell them not to. So long, Wendell."

"You are a goddamned idiot. That's what you are. Christ, Will, there's lots easier ways to commit suicide."

"Good-by, Wendell."

The old trail switchbacked down through a slot in the sandstone wall, passing beneath the last frontiers of the forest—scattered jackpines, a stand of Douglas fir in a shady corner of the wall, a clump of young aspens. Down into juniper and pinyon pine, an occasional agave, sagebrush, rabbit brush in summer bloom. A thousand feet of descent would bring him into a plant-life zone roughly equivalent to a journey five hundred miles southward. As he went down, the temperature, even before dawn, went up. In the bottom of the canyon it would be 120 degrees or more.

As he descended, picking his way slowly and carefully across the tumbled rocks and gravel of washouts, Gatlin checked each possible ledge where anyone could have made even a short traverse. He had little hope of finding her tracks, if she had come this way; the storm two days before would have obliterated all such signs, even as it had wrecked portions of the trail. But there was always the fractional chance that she might have sought refuge under some overhang, been trapped by a rockfall, been cut off, injured. A hundred different things could have happened and he intended to explore each separate possibility. In her distracted state of mind she could have gone anywhere, indeed, and of all choices a hike into the canyon at this time of year was the most unreasonable. But if she had gone to the mountains or to the city she was probably well, at least safe; if she had gone down into the canyon she was probably in trouble, if still alive. So Gatlin reasoned, anyway. Her young man, Larry the flyboy, Lawrence J. Turner III, cadet-pilot, USAF, had on the other hand gone off in a frenzy in all directions: flying to her parents in Washington and back; hiring a plane and nearly killing himself winging through the inner gorge at 150 miles an hour; wandering into the forest and almost getting lost himself; until now, exhausted and paralyzed, he simply sat and waited in Sandy's little apartment in the village, dreaming? praying? hoping? for her return. For Gatlin, at their last encounter, he had had no words; he regarded Gatlin as a murderer, or perhaps as something worse.

A mile below the rim, on the first of the lateral benches above the red wall, Gatlin stopped to cache two of the extra water jugs he carried, placing them under a ledge, hiding them with stones, inscribing the location on his memory.

The sun rose out of the desert far beyond and glared through unclouded sky into the canyon. The heat intensified immediately.

Gatlin hiked westward on the horizontal bench, following no trail—for there was no trail here, only a maze of faint deer paths which meandered in all directions, petering out in rock and brush—until he came to the point where the bench merged with the main canyon wall, a vertical drop-off of hundreds of feet, beyond which only the birds and the lizards could go.

Noon. Around him lay shallow potholes in the solid rock which two days before might have been full of water; now they were empty, sucked dry by the arid winds, the thirsty air. He crawled into the meager shade of a juniper, removed the pack, finished his first quart of water, ate some raisins and jerky. He was not hungry. He unlaced his boots, loosened his clothing, pillowed his head on the pack bag and tried to sleep. He could not sleep.

Nevertheless he forced himself to stay there in the shade till midafternoon. He then returned by a different, lower route to the trail and the place where he had cached the water. From there he traversed the bench eastward as far as it went, returning through twilight, again by a different route, to the starting point. On each leg of the hike he looked into every possible cranny in the rock big enough to conceal a human body. Found nothing, nothing but the homes of pack rats, the antlers of a buck, the marks of bobcat, coyote, lizards and rattlesnakes in the dust. On the way he drank nearly all of the water he carried. He had to drink it, or give up. Even the relative coolness after sundown was not sufficient to allay his body's greed—and need—for water.

Near the trail, as stars began to appear, he made camp for the night, brushing off a level place for his poncho and blanket, scraping together a few twigs and sticks for a little fire, on which he made tea and a thick soup. He still did not feel actually hungry, but he compelled himself to eat. He was tired, very tired, and thirsty again after eating. He drank the tea and set his canteen close to his bed, knowing that he would wake up during the night craving water.

Letting the fire die, he wrapped himself in the blanket, clasped his hands under his head and stared up at the stars. He thought he would fall asleep at once but he did not.

A bird called to him, off in the dusk.

"Will. Will. Poor-will."

Answered by another in a different direction.

"Poor-will. Poor-will. Poor-will."

Something woke him in the middle of the night. He opened his eyes to see a coyote watching him from ten feet away, standing sideways, head turned, staring at him with a curiosity which seemed almost sympathetic. Yet it was a lean, haggard beast, with the long muzzle of a wolf, and gleaming teeth. Gatlin stared back at the animal, plain enough in the starlight. Satisfied, not intimidated, the coyote after a time left off, turned and trotted away. Gatlin reached for the canteen.

His internal alarm woke him before dawn, when a faint reflected glow in the western sky made it appear that the sun had reversed its course or the earth had begun a counter rotation. All the familiar constellations were down. In this half-light he pulled on his boots, again made tea, and ate for breakfast a dense compound of cereals, nuts, dried fruit and wheat germ, mixed with powdered milk and water.

A corona of light appeared on the east, again in a sky unflawed by a trace of cloud. Gatlin removed one of the water jugs from his cache, refilled his canteens and packed them. He cleaned cup and spoon with his tongue.

The sun was still below the horizon. Gatlin found a sharp stone and dug a hole in the gravelly soil about two feet deep and three feet in diameter. He knocked the fat pads off some prickly pear, pushed them into the hole and cut them up into chunks with the stone. He set the empty water jug, without its lid, in the center of the hole, pushing it down among the broken pads of the cactus. He took a sheet of thin plastic from his pack, stretched it over the hole and fixed it in place with the material he had removed in making the hole, sealing the edges with dirt and sand. He worked slowly and easily, losing no sweat in the cool air of morning. With the transparent sheet firmly in place, he put one round stone in the center of it; the plastic sagged a little beneath the weight, forming an inverted cone with its apex directly over the mouth of the water jug. If he returned this way there would be, he hoped, enough water in the jug, distilled by the sun, to get him up the last mile to the rim.

The other jug, yet full, he packed in his bag, and shouldered pack and frame, buckled the waist strap and started down the trail.

The sun came up.

He reached the top of the Red Wall, a limestone cliff seven hundred feet high which paralleled the course of the canyon for most of its length. Through a fault in this structure, zigzagging down a talus of broken rock, the trail dropped to the world below, a broad gray platform halfway between rim and river, which also followed the windings of the canyon for over a hundred miles. Beyond this platform lay the inner gorge, a defile so deep and narrow that the river which ran through its depths could not be seen from where Gatlin stood.

He descended, feeling the heat rise and the aridity increase with each downward step.

The sun was high when he came to the end of the lowest switchback in the Red Wall and stepped out onto the rolling ground of the bench. Again he paused to cache a water jug, his last full gallon. As he had done the day before, he left the trail to make a traverse to the west, following as closely as he could the base of the limestone cliff. But this time he would go much farther.

He was now in a gray and barren region of saltbush, blackbrush, cactus and little else. There were no trees, not even the scrubbiest of junipers, nothing but the knee-high brush, the dusty desert, the pale glaring stone which made his squinting eyes burn and ache. Even here, however, were signs of animal life: snakes, lizards, birds, the twisting pathways of wild burros. But no trace of what he was searching for.

What did he really expect to find? A footprint, a message in a log, a scrap of tartan plaid on a thornbush, a faded picture? A broken body draped on rock, a thin cry for help? He knew that the possibility of any of these things was too small to measure, to make sense. His descent into this inferno was itself an act of insanity. Yet he could not have imagined doing anything else, any less. He trudged on under the cliff, under the blaze of the soaring sun.

When the heat became too great, as it finally did, he crept on hands and knees under the overhang of a boulder into a dusty, scat-littered den which might have been the home of coyote or lion. Wearily, shakily, he undid the pack and drew out a canteen and drank deeply, desperately, letting the warm good water course down his throat as if he could never get enough, as if every cell in his body was demanding the liquid of life. When he finally had all that he needed he stretched out in the dust, head on the pack, and closed his eyes. Outside, in the fierce light, a lizard scurried by, dragging its whiplike tail; locusts screamed from the burning brush. Far above, against the blue, a single vulture gyred through space, black wings motionless, and scanned the desert below with magnetic vision—those protruding eyes socketed in the red raw naked flesh of the beaked head.

"Will, wake up!"

She was laughing at him, shaking him gently, her eyes bright with gaiety. The long hair, shining like burnished copper, fragrant as cliff rose, hung across her bare shoulders and trailed in his face. He could smell the perfume of her breasts, taste the sweetness of her arms.

He opened his eyes.

Strands of a cobweb tickled his face. A few inches from his nose a spider, gray as the dust, dangled from the overhanging rock, extruding from its abdomen a hairlike filament of spume. Instinctively, with a shudder of revulsion, Gatlin brushed away both web and spider and rolled out of the den. He looked at the sun. He had slept for nearly two hours and felt the pang of loss, the bewildering pain of something precious, beautiful, irreplaceable swept away forever.

He also felt, at once, the need for water. He drank, emptying one of his two canteens. Then relaced his boots, put on the pack and his hat, and started off again, following an ancient burro path. He staggered a little at first, dazed by sleep, weakened and confused by the heat. But recovered, marched on, feeling his strength and purpose begin to return.

All through the afternoon he trudged toward the sun, into the evening, into the magenta obscurity which followed sundown, until he was forced to halt by the growing darkness. In the sand of a nearby ravine, among boulders and burned-out brittlebush, he dug for water but found none. He opened the other canteen, drank, built a small fire and fixed himself a supper, ate what he could. He licked his cup and spoon dry.

Very tired, stunned by despair, he lay in the blanket and gazed up at the constellations, those glittering chains which enmeshed the sky. The extravagant randomness of their distribution puzzled the will. All space was charged with their inaudible vibrations. (Inaudible, that is, to the unaided ear. Had he not heard often enough, late at night on the shortwave radio, the siren song of Venus? the deep drone of Jupiter? the fanatic signals from beyond Saturn? Or was it merely fancy to imagine that all of those, all of that which seemed so incomprehensibly remote was actually enclosed by his own consciousness? In the madness, the exultation of solar winds? In the heart-chilling bleakness of his own inmost sensations? his outermost thoughts?)

A blue-green meteor slashed down through the tail of Scorpio, melted into nothing.

His life melted into dreams.

Tortured by thirst, he crawled toward the final resource he had prepared days before, the disc of silver gleaming under the fire of the sun. He neared the place, came upon it, eagerly removed the dirt and sand and lifted the transparent sheet. Instead of water he saw a nest of scorpions, a writhing mass which squirmed, piled, crawled upon itself, multiplying as he watched, there in the pit.

He came to the second secret place, exhausted, hopeless; he brushed away the seal and raised a corner of the clear plastic. And what he found here was not water but a giant rose, a rose nested within a rose, a score of roses sparkling with dew, sweeter than love, inviting him down, down, into the nectar of their hearts. As he entered they parted before him, petals like portals opening before him, closing behind, drawing him deeper into another world, down a brown road that wound among strange green vine-covered hills, toward a tall and weathered farmhouse where his mother waited, his father, his brothers. They would all be glad to see him, he thought, at the end of this journey which had taken so much longer than anyone could have imagined; already he could envision the timid, unbelieving, miracle-struck smile that would glow like sunlight on his mother's gothic face. But the road had taken a different turning; instead of a farmhouse was a crescent blaze of shore and sea, a deserted coast where no ships came, where no man lived, where no wings wove invisible patterns through the air. Only the waves advanced and retreated, with gush of foam and slide of surf upon the sleek sands, on a beach beneath a cliff where the skeleton of a home now stood, the barren timbers never sheathed in walls, unroofed, never completed; through the framework of this house, as if looking through an iron grid, he saw the pale sky, the concentric coronets of dawn, the flames and disc of the rising sun.

Waking once again, he was struck nerveless, drawn hollow by the horror of his deprivation. By the senseless sudden blackness of her vanishing.

Lacking appetite, he ate little, drank half of what water he still had left and turned back toward the east, taking a different track across the middle of the vast and open desert below the cliffs, above the inner canyon. Searching for a shred of cloth, the imprint of a girl's foot, a sign of meaning, he found only the maze of paths made by the feral burros among the brush and rocks, and the winding trail of reptiles in the dust.

By noon he was out of water. As before, he rested, or attempted to rest, in the shade of a ledge during the worst hours of the afternoon. Later, after dark, when he came finally to the canyon trail and his water cache he was seriously dehydrated, ill. Anxiously he uncovered the remaining water jug, opened it with trembling, enfeebled fingers and drank. Drank till his belly could hold no more, till the insistent craving of the body was satisfied. He filled his two canteens with the water left in the jug, draining it, and planted it in a hole in the ground as he had done the other, mashing cactus pads around it and stretching a second sheet of transparent plastic over the opening. In the morning he would have to go down to the river. Hungry again, he cooked himself a supper and went to sleep.

All through the next day and the day that followed he hiked along the river, climbing up and down the taluses of debris, trudging over sand dunes, forcing a way through mesquite thickets and tangles of acacia. At midday he stripped and cooled himself in the water; found refuge from the sun and the 120-degree heat in the shade of boulders; made his way around dark crevices in the rock where dun-colored diamondbacks lay coiled, regarding his passage with lidless eyes and black flickering tongues, their rattles whirring like choruses of locusts. The lizards darted out of his way—whiptails, geckos, collared lizards, fat chuckwallas that hissed and blinked and inflated themselves to grotesque proportions, meant as menace. He passed the tunnels of tarantulas; he saw now and then a centipede, a scorpion, a solpugid. He found nothing that could interest him.

On the first of his two nights by the river he made camp near a rapids. The smoke of his fire mixed with spray from the thundering river. Even in the dark he could see the waters crashing over the drop-off, piling up in ten-foot waves against the granite fangs below, hissing past the ledge on shore. The foam of the tumbled water glowed with spectral luminosity in the darkness, under the stars. The white roar filled his dreams all night long.

The second night he slept on a beach. Here the river was quiet, tons of silty water flowing by each second with no more noise than a distant buried dynamo might make —the sound of power, smooth, assured, unfaltering. Above the river on either side stood the black cliffs of polished schist and granite, Precambrian, Archean, more ancient than anything else on the surface of the earth. And here his dreams were haunted by the silence.

Early the next morning he prepared to climb to the desert again, the middle world between the river below and the forested plateau above. He compelled himself to eat a big breakfast; he drank all the water he could hold, mixing it with powdered fruit juice. He filled his canteens and packed them and filled also a pair of plastic bags which he could carry in his hands. He hunted for the foot of the old trail, long out of use, which would lead him up to the bench.

The trail was hard to follow, washed out completely in many places; it took him half the day to reach the desert platform above the inner gorge. On the way, scrambling across taluses of debris, he broke one of the water bladders. The sun blazed through the pure sky; the canyon walls reflected and radiated heat; in the distance, headwalls and pinnacles swayed dreamily behind a film of heat waves. The rock was almost too hot to touch with his bare hand, it burned through the soles of his boots. At noon he sought shelter from the sun but there was none; he kept climbing until he was able to find a little shade under an overhang at the head of a ravine. He stopped and squatted under the rock—there was not room enough to lie down—and waited through the next three hours.

Half his water was already gone; he opened one of the canteens.

Waiting there, half asleep on his heels, stupefied by heat and exhaustion, he stared at a buzzard circling in the sky off to the west. One black shape floating in the air, around and around in endless lazy circles. The glare of the sunlight made his eyes ache; he closed them, lowered his head and tried to sleep.

The next time he looked there were three vultures soaring where only one had been before. Instead of rising with the thermal updrafts and drifting on, as they usually did, the birds were gradually descending, in cautious spirals, toward some attraction on the ground.

Gatlin roused himself. He crept out of the shade and willed his body upright. He shouldered the pack frame, put on his hat, climbed out of the ravine and hiked toward the disappearing birds, following the contour of the slope below the red wall. As he made his way among the rocks, skirting prickly pear and thornbush, he saw more black wings appear in the sky. The gathering of the clan. Whatever it was they were coming down for was hidden from him by the successive dips and rises of the terrain. It was impossible for him, in the heat, in his fatigue, to run over the broken ground; but he hastened forward, sliding and stumbling down into one gulch after another, scrambling up the far side and hurrying on. His shirt turned dark with sweat. Tears, of which he was unaware, streamed through the stubble of beard on his face. He groaned, gasped for breath, clawing at the brush and loose stones as he struggled up the final incline and reached the crest.

At first he saw only a mass of black feathers, a cluster of bald red heads. The vultures were so engrossed in their meal they did not immediately notice the man on the skyline above them. He rushed down, they raised their dripping beaks, vomited, scattered, beating the air with long and heavy wings, and skipped nimbly into space.

Halfway down the slope Gatlin stopped. The quarry was only a deer, a small doe battered and partly dismembered by a long fall from the cliff above. He turned aside, stumbling slowly toward the nearest patch of shade, and rested for an hour. He drank a great deal of water, emptying the first canteen. In the sky the vultures soared and reassembled and after a while the boldest of them ventured to begin to descend. They were all feeding by the time Gatlin found the strength to resume his march.

The sun, touching the horizon, burned for a few minutes directly into his face. He paused to rest, turning his back on the glare, and gazed with weary, aching, blood-flecked eyes at the world of the canyon.

He was alone in one of the loneliest places on earth. Above him rose tier after tier of cliffs, the edge of the forest barely apparent on the rim of the uppermost wall; around him the gray desert platform where nothing grew but scrub brush and cactus sloped toward the brink of the inner gorge and the unseen river. From river to forest an ascent of over five thousand feet; from rim to rim ten miles by airline at the most narrow point; from canyon head to canyon mouth two hundred and eighty-five miles by the course of the river. In all this region was nothing human that he could see, no sign of man or of man's work. No sign, no trace, no path, no clue, no person but himself.

Alone. Was he alone?

"Sandy!" he howled. And waited for an answer.

After a moment the cliffs answered. One, then a second, then a third, and more:

    SANDY
        Sandy
            sandy . . .

Echo answered echo, fading out in delicate diminuendo through league on league of empty space, a wave of sound whose farthest ripple died unheard in the twilight air, on the farthest shore of canyon and desert:

> *sandy*
>   *sandy*
>   *sandy* . . .

38   Dear Willy,

Receipt of your recent monosyllabic communication is hereby gratefully acknowledged. Yes, since you are so good, I shall come. I shall overcome.

Somehow I gather from a certain "aura" surrounding your "letter" that you have perhaps finally had about enough of solitude, the forest, reverie, and other forms of autoerotic madness. I trust that this means I may succeed in luring you with me back to the life of the world, back to the students who need you, the women who will love you, the men who will both hate and admire you. Believe me, lad, they all need you. As you need them. As we all need each other.

As for my personal affairs, they follow their customary course, up hill and down, from heaven to hell and back, round and round with faithless Fortuna's turning wheel. Darnelle has left me again, this time for good. No matter; another will soon take her place. I love them all, friend Will, or at least I love all that are lovable. Is it not, after all, the love that matters and not the object?

Love wells up within me like an irrepressible spring; and my love for women increases my fraternity with men.

I have abandoned my schemes for socialized civic whorehouses, which I believe I elaborated for you in one of my previous letters, as too . . . well, schematic. Too formal, doctrinaire, cold, commercial. And not necessary. In my present rosy optimism, good old Will, I believe that we in this crazy tragic splendid society are working our way, with much agony and confusion to be sure, toward something entirely new, a kind of world community now barely imaginable, in which men and women will pass freely and happily from one to another, as they choose, bouncing from one jolly romance to another as freely as the birds, choosing new mates each season. I foresee true community, Will, true intercommunication, true brotherhood, sisterhood, comradeship, a great big global *kibbutz*.

As for children, now the chief victims of this agonizing transitional period, I see children becoming (through systematic population control) less commonplace than they now are and consequently much more valuable, prized darlings of entire communities, each child surrounded by the love not merely of its mother and father but also of a hundred grandfathers and grandmothers, a thousand aunts and uncles. In a true community, if we can achieve such a thing, each child shall be the child of all.

No doubt you'll think this a foolish utopianism. But my God, Willy, I think now that we've got to go all out, once and for all, toward the new world. Or else perish in black reaction, war and tyranny. Revolution is in the air, lad, the slaves are rising everywhere, the young are crying out for change, are demanding change, are throwing their very bodies against the levers of the old rusty iron machinery of authority and hierarchy and privilege. We must join them, Willy, aid them, guide them in so far as we can.

Ah well . . . it's far too much for a letter. I'm taking

the fall quarter off, will spend a couple weeks with you in the October woods, we'll talk the whole thing through.

I see by the papers you're having an exciting time out there this year. An airplane crash, a rash of forest fires, a priest and a boy found dead of thirst down in the canyon. How many victims now? Did they ever find that girl who was supposed to have disappeared a couple of years ago? Did she even exist?

Anyway, see you soon, old comrade. Will be a great pleasure to talk with you once again. And believe me: *all will be well among the glorious elect!*
—Red Dog the Hopeful

39

THEY KNELT side by side on the white marble ledge, peering down into the pool. The water was deep, dark and still as glass, perhaps bottomless, and like a mirror reflected their naked bodies—his brown, broad, shaggy-haired; hers fair and slim, soft, vulnerable. (The flowing hair; the innocence of her delicate pink-tipped breasts.) They smiled at each other in this mirror of water. Above, or below, or beyond their reflections lay the deep and flowing sky, empty of all but a trace of cloud and the glow of the approaching sun. Sunlight shone through her hair as the racing sun rose behind their shoulders, cleared the shadow of the rock, and burst with a flare of fire into the center of the mirror—a blinding and terrible beauty which obliterated everything but the image of itself.

40

BALLANTINE is still sleeping. In the blue dawn Gatlin loads his rifle, levels it across the windowsill, through the open cabin window, and waits for the deer.

Waiting, he sips coffee, warming his cold right hand and trigger finger on the hot mug. His exhaling breath turns to vapor in the chilly air near the window. Outside, on the grass of the clearing, is a sheen of hoarfrost. Beyond the clearing stands the aspen glade, the tall slender white trunks crowned with masses of golden leaves thin as foil and mobile, trembling all together in the faintest motion of the air. Beyond the aspens are the dark forms of spruce and fir. The forest is quite silent.

Within the cabin the fire in the cookstove makes a purring, crackling noise; the old cast iron of the stove expands with a sound of clicks and clinks, almost as steady as a watch; and from the single cot against the wall come the irregular half-smothered snores of sleeping Ballantine, buried in his downy mummybag.

A harsh awakening, thinks Gatlin. And a harsh going into sleep. As Ballantine comes suddenly awake a deer will be dying. He drinks the hot coffee. The rifle is cocked, ready. Steadily, without wavering, he watches the clearing, the wall of the forest.

But the deer are already there. He does not see them come but there they are, four of them, a heavy-antlered buck and three young does, magically present where nothing but nothingness had been a moment before. They approach slowly, tentatively, stopping to look and listen after each step, as if aware of a menace in this place which was not here before. All but the old buck appear sleek, glossy-coated, fat from a summer of good feeding.

Ignoring the buck, Gatlin takes aim on the nearest of the three does quartering across his field of fire, aligning his sights on a point close behind the shoulder, near the crest of the spine—instant extinction of consciousness. The doe, presenting her flank, continues to move. Gatlin swings the muzzle of the rifle to follow, and the deer, sensing this almost imperceptible adjustment, come to a halt, all four, and stare directly at him.

They stare at him, the great ears up and alert, the large and protruding eyes dark, shining, suggesting more a look of wonder and surprise than of fear.

Gatlin shifts his bead from the spine to the forehead of his target, not more than fifty feet away. Between the eyes. Relaxed, not breathing, he begins to squeeze the trigger. The doe gazes back at him, straight across the blackened open sights, into his face. Intensely alert, poised for instant flight, she seems nevertheless not afraid. The end of her world lies no further away than the tension of a spring, the millimetric thrust of the firing pin. She waits, staring at the clean clear forms of things, which all converge upon one center within one focus of a consciousness.

Gatlin lets out the trigger, draws the rifle back across the sill. The deer spring away and vanish. For a while he sits there, idle, then takes the prop out from under the sash and lowers the window, unloads the rifle and slides it into its case. Stoking the fire, he adds fuel, slides the big skillet into place.

"Art," he calls. No response. "Art," he calls again, gently, putting a hand on Ballantine's shoulder through the folds of the bag. "Let's get out of here today. Time to go."

After breakfast they prepare for departure. Part of his property Gatlin has taken down the trail to his truck the day before; the remainder—bedroll, rifle, cooking gear, food, soap and comb and towel and such—he will pack down today. He climbs the tower for the last time but not to look for smoke; half the forest is already under snow, the southern mountains are covered with snow, and all of the fire-fighting crew are now gone. Everyone but Gatlin has gone; the lodge closed down, the rangers transferred to their winter stations, the entrance road officially closed. Gatlin disconnects the radio set, lowers the aerial and stows it inside, closes the shutters over the windows, locks the door. About to descend, he notices the sky, solidly overcast from horizon to horizon, gray and somber with the premonition of more snow, of winter, scored across its southerly hemisphere with a track of pearly light—progress of the hidden, reeling sun.

Ballantine now has a pack on his back, waiting. Gatlin closes up the cabin, shutters the windows, damps out the fire in the stove, caps the chimney. He is ready to go. He straps on his pack. Together they walk down the leaf-covered pathway under the shivering, whispering aspen trees. Down through the crooked grove.

"Coming back?"

"Never."

"You don't seem much troubled about it."

"I'm not."

Most of the time during the walk they are silent. For Ballantine, a strange silence. For Gatlin, after a week of dialogue, welcome. The forest is also silent. The birds are gone, the squirrels hiding, the deer keep out of sight. They come to the foot of the trail and unload their burdens into the back of Gatlin's pickup truck. He removes a power saw from the pile of baggage in the truck bed, covers and secures everything else under a tarpaulin.

"What's that for?"

"Part of the job. I get paid for it. You'll see."

They get in the truck, drive down the dirt road to its junction with the paved road which leads in one direction to a dead end at the lodge and village now closed for the winter, in the other direction out to the highway and the towns and the world of men.

Here Gatlin stops the truck. He starts the motor of the power saw, a snarling racket in the autumn stillness, and notches and fells a pair of tall aspens across the dirt road. He does the same at the paved road, blocking it with tree trunks.

"Won't the snow be enough to keep anyone out?"

"When it comes, yes. But it ain't here yet."

Gatlin puts the power saw back in the truck. Ballantine gets into the cab. Gatlin walks off for a moment, toward an ancient log that lies in the brush near the junction of the two roads. Taking a pen and notebook from his pocket he scribbles something on a page of the notebook, a single word, tears out the page and folds and stuffs it into an opening near the base of the log. Returning quickly to the truck, he gets in and starts the engine. Ballantine stares at him.

"What were you doing at that log?"

Gatlin drives toward the highway, says nothing.

"Okay, don't tell me. I know you're crazy anyway so what does it matter. Let's get out of here."

Gatlin stops three times more to fell trees across the road. Then they come to a locked gate. He has the key. He drives through and relocks the gate, on which the sign says ROAD CLOSED. Beyond the gate is the main highway, leading east and west, and an outpost of commerce—gas station, cafe, motel. They stop, go in the cafe for lunch.

The place is almost empty, since the tourist season is over and the deer season not yet (officially) begun. A truckdriver sits at one end of the counter, a highway patrolman at the other. Ballantine and Gatlin sit in a booth beside the window. Ballantine tries to make conversation but finds it hard going with his unresponsive companion. He is obviously relieved, delighted when a girl comes to wait on them.

The girl. Bold green eyes made doubly large and bold with eye shadow and mascara. Flaxen hair, glossy and long, and bright white teeth within a cool smile. The arms bare, glowing with health and golden down; the swell of her bosom under the close-fitting black frock . . . like all of them, she is beautiful.

"Hello," says Ballantine. "Who are you?"

She gives him her sly, ironic smile. "Claire."

"Claire. Claire. That means light."

"Yes, it does. Do you want to see the menu?"

"No, no. I want to see—light."

The girl turns to Gatlin, who sits staring out the window at the forest under its heavy sky. His hands are interlocked, he says nothing. She opens her lips, about to speak.

"Yes," Ballantine says, "bring us the menu. Your name is really Claire?"

"Yes sir."

"Why, you could be the light of my life."

"Could be." But the girl is looking at Gatlin, not at Ballantine.

He glances up at her for a moment, then continues gazing out at the trees.

Ballantine laughs. "Okay," he says, "and bring us each a bottle of beer."

"Sir?" She hadn't heard him.

"Hemlock," he says. "A cup of hemlock."

"Hemlock?"

"I'm kidding, sweetheart." With a smile on his hand-

some, ruddy face, Ballantine repeats the original order. The girl leaves. Ballantine faces his friend.
"Will?" he says.
The other stares out the window, into the forest.
"Will," says Ballantine.